Fast Bytes

W9-DCB-812

Digital Photography

Nina Martini

DATA BECKER®

Contents

Controlling the print quality: Calibrating the monitor and printer **141**

Connecting and transferring data

Fortunately, transferring your newly taken snapshots to a computer has become more and more convenient recently due to advancements such as USB interfaces and Firewire. In this chapter you learn about basics such as power consumption and storage media, transferring images onto the computer, and copying and renaming images. In addition, you find an overview of the most important file formats.

Tip

Preventing scratches by using self-made display protection

Because display screens are delicate, it is advisable to protect them from scratches. You can use adhesive films or Plexiglas films for this purpose. You might also want to go to a specialty store to enquire about protective films that can be easily removed again – or test the film on a similar surface before you apply it to the display screen. This way you can exchange the protective film without damaging the display screen.

Removing scratches from LCD monitors

There is a simple solution if your LCD monitor is accidentally scratched: Ask your cell phone dealer or watchmaker about special LCD polish. These polishes are about $5.00 and remove fine scratches in no time at all.

Power consumption

You must consider power consumption because digital cameras clearly consume more power than 35mm cameras. Manufacturers cannot specify in minutes how long power supplies will last because the electric power consumption depends on the display runtime, flash use, playing with the functions, data storage and data transfer. It therefore makes sense to operate digital cameras with rechargeable batteries. In case you are frequently using the camera for stationary purposes, it might also be worthwhile to acquire an adapter. Nowadays, a set of batteries as well as the appropriate charger is usually included when purchasing a digital camera. Also consider the following point when purchasing the device: With some types of cameras, all dates and time settings are lost once the camera's batteries are entirely empty. Other camera types can prevent this loss by using separate button cell batteries. This does not apply to the photos that are saved on your camera – they remain saved and are available to you.

1. Connecting and transferring data

Summary of the most important power supplies

	Alkaline batteries	Nickel Cadmium batteries (NiCD)	Nickel Metal Hydride batteries (NiMH)	Lithium Ion batteries
Description	These are the popular batteries in Mignon size.	Nickel Cadmium batteries have been the leading type of batteries for a long time.	The Nickel Metal Hydride batteries are one most recommendable type of batteries.	This is a perfect battery pack for digital cameras and camcorders. At the same capacity, the pack is a lot smaller than Mignon batteries.
Advantages	Because these batteries are used with many devices, they are available in almost any country.	This type of battery is not harmed by strong fluctuations of temperature.	This type distinguishes itself through its high storage capacity. In addition, the dreaded memory effect does not take place.	Of all the battery types mentioned here, lithium ion battery packs offer the highest storage capacity.
Disadvantages	This type of battery is not rechargable. This means that in the long term, they are more expensive and have a greater environmental impact.	With this type of battery, you encounter the memory effect. The batteries "remember" if they were not sufficiently discharged before recharging them. In the meantime this decreases the capacity, which is not restorable. The capacity of this type of battery is comparetively low.	The purchasing cost of this type of battery is somewhat higher than with Nickel Cadmium batteries. Attention: These batteries are susceptible to over-charging. You therefore require a "smart" charger, which fully discharges the batteries first and automatically turns itself off once the batteries are fully charged.	The purchase price of this battery type is a lot higher than the price of other batteries.

When choosing your power supply, always pay attention to the information provided by the manufacturer. It is important to know that (generally) you should not use no zinc coal batteries.

Storage media

Huge quantities of data might accrue when saving digital images. Each image pixel has to be described. Therefore, choosing the right storage medium is one of the most important decisions in digital photography. Your needs might grow fast, and you might also want to shoot all of your pictures at the highest possible resolution to obtain the best quality. Storage media can be looked at as the "film" for your digital camera. You are introduced to the most important ones in this chapter.

Preventing the loss of data stored on your camera

You should always turn off your camera before exchanging batteries or connecting the camera to the wall power supply. Otherwise, a malfunction could result, and, although it's rare to lose all of the data stored in the camera, it is possible.

Memory Stick

The memory stick is a compact and robust medium and therefore convenient. On the back of the stick, notice a small mechanical erasure prevention switch, which is similar to the one you know from 3.5 inch diskettes. This switch prevents the accidental over-writing or deletion of data. To transfer data to a PC or notebook, use a floppy disk adapter (approximately US$50.00), a PC card adapter (approximately US$60.00; prices can vary greatly - *www.pcworld.com; www.kingston.com/ flash/pcread.asp*) as well as separate card readers (approximately US$70.00) that work through a USB connection. Unfortunately, the memory stick can hardly be used with anything but Sony devices so far. The good thing is that the stick can be used with digital cameras, photo printers, walkmans, mobile phones, dictaphones, and video cameras made by this manufacturer.

SmartMedia

SmartMedia cards are half the size of a bank card and have a depth of less than one millimeter. The area of contact is exposed on the surface, and therefore the card can

be damaged pretty easily. Unfortunately, this small medium does not contain any electronic circuitry to control the storage. For this reason, SmartMedia cards are dependent on the devices they are used with. The card also has the disadvantage that image and music data cannot be saved on one medium because it has to be formatted differently depending on the type of application. In case you are thinking of getting this medium, you should definitely seek advice to find out whether it is useful for the kind of applications you want to use it for – or whether you should use Compact Flash instead.

SD Memory Card

The SD memory card is future friendly because soon entire gigabytes are supposed to fit on this small medium. You can use SD memory cards for audio players, organizers, cell phones, or digital cameras. In comparison to SmartMedia, this card has the advantage that the area of contact is more protected. In addition, the card contains the required electronics to make it device-independent. Furthermore, the data transfer is particularly fast. SD memory cards also offer a security feature for the protection of copyrights – it does not protect copyrighted MP3 files, however.

Compact Flash

You can also use Compact Flash cards with different media devices such as MP3 players and organizers. When purchasing such a card, take into consideration that cards are of different thicknesses. Ensure that the card you buy is compatible with your device. Cards of up to one GB storage capacity are already available. This storage medium also contains the electronic technology necessary to make it device-independent. PC card adapters and external reading devices are available to transfer data.

Microdrive

If you are shooting at a high resolution and consequently have to manage high quantities of data, the microdrive is the perfect solution for you. The microdrive is an actual, tiny hard disk. It is exceptionally fast and already saves up to one GB; however, it also requires a lot of power. You can transfer the data through a USB connection, a PC card adapter, or a CompactFlash II reading device.

As with most of the other media, you can also use microdrives for organizers and MP3 player.

Overview of storage media

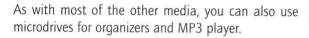

Medium	Memory Stick	SmartMedia	SD Memory Card	Compact Flash	Microdrive
Functionality	Flash Memory	Flash Memory	Flash Memory	Flash Memory	Hard disk technology
Capacity (in MB)	4, 8, 16, 32, 64	4, 8, 16, 32, 64, 128	4, 8, 16, 32, 64 (available) 128, 256 (2001) to 1 GB (2002)	8, 16, 32, 48, 64, 96, 128, 160, 256, 512	340, 512, 1024
Advantages	small medium sufficient capacity	small format high capacity can be used with many devices good value for money	small format high capacity	small format high capacity can be used with many devices maximum capacity hardware-independent good value for money	favorable price per MB high capacity can be used with many devices
Disadvantages	Music data is encrypted can only be used with Sony devices	maximum capacity dependent on hardware	data is encrypted not widespread yet		mechanical parts adapter required often, requires a lot of power

Editing video sequences

Many cameras offer the possibility of recording video sequences. Often, only short sequences such as one-minute-long scenes, for instance, can be recorded. If you are using powerful storage media, however, you can record a number of sequences one after the other. You can then edit these scenes with video editing software such as Ulead's VideoStudio.

Transferring your images

If you haven't yet decided to work with a reading device for external media, you can transfer the images directly from your camera to your PC to edit, archive, and print them.

The first connection

Fortunately, the transfer process has been made relatively easy with the development of USB interfaces and the most recent operating systems. Every camera manufacturer provides different software with the device; therefore, a universal description of the transfer process cannot be offered here. The different transfer procedures are similar, however. Consequently, a camera by Minolta is used here to illustrate the individual steps.

Adapter for stationary operation

Because the transfer requires a lot of power, use a power adapter. Remember, data loss might occur if the current flow of the battery is interrupted during the data transfer process.

1 First, start your computer before you connect the camera.

2 Make sure that the camera contains the desired medium such as a Compact Flash card.

3 Switch your camera to PC mode and then turn it on. This particular sequence of steps is important.

4 Connect the broader plug of the connecting cable with the corresponding socket on the camera.

5 Connect the other end of the cable with the computer.

6 Your operating system now recognizes the camera and asks you to insert the corresponding installation CD when you connect the camera for the first time.

7 Select your CD drive in the wizard and acknowledge the dialog box. The wizard now guides you through the installation procedure. Confirm the corresponding dialog boxes.

8 If you open your desktop now, your camera is indicated by a new icon for the data exchange medium.

9 You can treat your camera like a regular drive now. Copy the data into an image directory by using Explorer.

Firewire jack and connector - these interfaces were developed by Apple and are frequently used for professional digital cameras.

Renaming images automatically

Your digital camera consecutively numbers the recorded images. If you transfer these images to your computer and don't rename them afterwards, you might mix them up later when you transfer images the next time. You can use the image viewer ACDSee to change the image descriptions of particular images or of an entire folder at once. You can download this program from the following Web page: *http:// www.acdsystems.com*

1 Start ACDSee and switch to the directory in which you have copied your images – in this case *C:\Images Holiday.*

2 You can now select individual images by clicking them, pressing Ctrl and clicking further images. You can also select the command *Edit/Select All* from the main program menu.

> **Selecting images in ACDSee**
>
> You must click a spot within the Files window before you select the images. Once ADCSee selects the images, they appear with a blue border. If this is not the case, click one of the images in the window to the right and repeat *Edit/Select All*.

3 Select the commands *Edit/Batch Rename*. A dialog box opens that can be used to control the renaming procedure.

4 At this time, the images start with the designation PICT and are numbered with four digits. Replace PICT with the term Hawaii-Holiday, and replace the four-digit numbering with two-digit numbering. To do so, enter the term Hawaii-Holiday in the Template data-entry field and add two # symbols. This way ACDSee knows that two-digit numbering should be used after the Hawaii-Holiday designation.

5 In the lower section of the dialog box, all changes appear immediately. Confirm with *OK* if you are happy with the renaming results. The images are then permanently renamed.

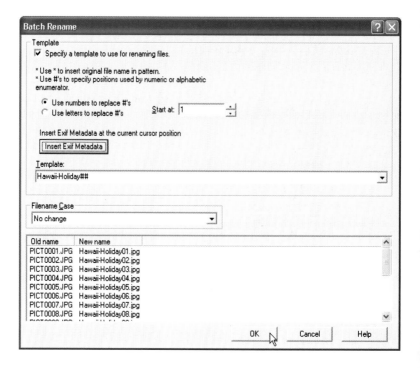

Tripods prevent blurry images

Even the steadiest hand fails when using long exposure times. If you work with long focal lengths or if you take close-ups and automatic release pictures as well as pictures requiring a long exposure time, find a steady surface to put your camera on. Frequently, auxiliary means such as a wall is sufficient; however, sometimes you should use a tripod. Many digital cameras contain a tripod thread to which any of the current tripods can be attached. You might also want to consider buying a panorama head with your tripod.

Digital zoom

The digital zoom function can be deceptive. With this kind of zooming, additional electronic pixels are added to the optical resolution of the camera. This process does not increase the quality, however. The additional pixels are added the same way – by means of interpolation – as in your image-editing software. If you want to enlarge your images, use ACDSee or Paint Shop Pro, for instance. This way, you save the memory space of your digital camera and the result is the same. As a rule, pictures should not be enlarged by more than 30%, as a certain loss in sharpness occurs at higher zoom factors due to the insertion of pixels. In this connection, the algorithms of digital cameras work in a similar manner. You can find a nice program on the Internet that promises almost loss-free enlargements. It's called S-Spline 2.0, and you can download free test versions from *http://www.shortcut.nl* for Macintosh computers as well as PCs. The trial version cannot save, however. It is therefore recommended you acquire the full version for US$69. The quality of the images that were enlarged with S-Spline strongly depends on the subject displayed in the image. Pictures containing many edges appear to be of a better quality than images with many details.

The most important file formats in digital photography

To save memory space, different methods of compression are used to remove unimportant or repeated image pixels that are inserted again during the decompression procedure. It is important to know that there are lossy and loss-free compression techniques. Images that are saved in loss-free formats can be opened, edited, and copied frequently. It is a different story with lossy compression techniques, however, such as the compression used with JPGs. These images should be saved only once or twice. Although better compression rates are obtained with these methods, it is not possible to reproduce the exact pixels of the original image when decompressing the image. Each time you resave the image, a loss in quality occurs.

In case you need to save lossy compression formats such as JPG a number of times, the maximum quality setting should be used to reduce the data loss to a minimum. Note: the higher the sharpness and amount of details in a picture, the worse the data reduction result is.

Tiff, uncompressed

Tiff, LZW compressed

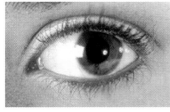

JPG, maximum quality

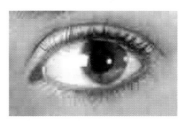

JPG, minimum quality

JPG JPEG compression is most suitable for images containing a lot of details. It works by separating luminance information and color information. JPG separates the image in rectangles that are 8 x 8 pixels in size and adjusts the color information. The higher the set compression level, the more visible the unattractive JPG artifacts are. This technique is not well suited for image files containing edges and text. The reduction in file size is considered a lossy compression – that is, it is not loss-free.

JPEG 2000 The revision of the JPEG standard promises a better image quality at higher compression rates. A pixel image is analyzed in detail before the compression, and single-colored sections are only resolved approximately. The occurrence of artifacts – the concise rectangular interferences – in JPEG images should be noticably reduced with this format.

BMP The Windows bitmap format can manage True Color, that is 16.7 millions of colors. BMP is the standard Windows bitmap format. If you save a file in this format, you can either save it in Microsoft Windows or OS/2 format and at a color depth between 1 to 24 bit. The RLE compression is available for 4 bit and 8 bit images, which is loss-free; however, drastically lower compression rates are obtained with it.

1. Connecting and transferring data

RAW   The RAW format manages the raw data of pictures and is mostly used in scientific areas. Because this format is not standardized, RAW files can usually be opened only with special software.

TIFF   The Tagged Image File format is one of the most popular image formats and is frequently used for transfers between image editing and layout programs. TIFF can handle true color mode as well as alpha channels to save selections. It is accepted by many service providers and recommended for most scanned images. With Tiff you have the option of using loss-free LZW compression. Images with large, single-color areas are suitable for compression.

PNG   Abbreviation for "portable network graphic format" (pronounced: ping). PNG was developed to replace GIF and JPEG images in the Internet. This format can compress without a heavy loss in quality. Like GIF, PNG can save transparency. PNG has the advantage, however, that transparency gradients can be implemented as PNG also supports alpha channels.

Optimizing images fast and easy

For its new 4.0 version, ACDSee has vamped itself up from the original image viewing program to an image-editing program. For complicated detail corrections and photo montages, you still need a program like Paint Shop Pro, but if you only want to rotate, crop, sharpen, or correct colors, ACDSee is all you need. You can find ACDSee at *http://www.acdsystems.com*. To obtain a free trial version of Paint Shop Pro, go to *http://www.jasc.com* and look for the *Free downloads* area.

On drive C, notice the folder entitled *Images*. The images in this directory have a multitude of problems: some pictures lack contrast and sharpness, some have to be rotated. One picture, for instance, has a strong color cast. All of these problems are resolved with ACDSee in this chapter.

2. Optimizing images fast and easy

1 When you open ACDSee, you find yourself in the regular view by default. This view allows you to navigate to your image folder or album on the left, while you can see the contents of the folder on the right. Underneath the directory panel, you can see the currently selected image in a magnified view.

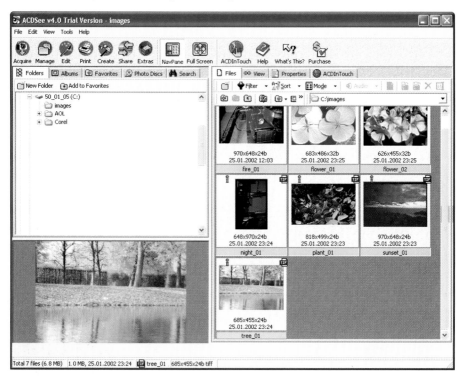

Switching between different views

Should your ACDSee display differ from the one illustrated here, you can change it by clicking one of these buttons. With the NavPane button you can view or hide the navigation panel on the left (when you hide the navigation panel, the magnified individual image preview at the bottom also disappears, however). With Full Screen, you can make maximum use of the screen size for your ACDSee display; however, the navigation panel and the large preview image also disappear in this mode. If you want to return from Full Screen view to the regular view, click the corresponding button in the upper right corner of the screen.

2 Depending where your pictures are saved, click one of the tabs at the top of the navigation panel. If you want to open a folder, click the *Folders* tab. Then select the directory and open the desired folder. The contents of the folder are then displayed on the right.

Images with depth

Depth is an important design element. When you take pictures, a three-dimensional scene is converted into a two-dimensional photograph. Give your photograph depth with the help of designing tricks. Make sure that large objects (for example, trees as well as streets or rails) that are at a certain distance from each other suggest three-dimensionality.

Rotating pictures

Depending on whether you have taken landscape or portrait-oriented pictures, you might have to rotate some of your pictures. In the *Images* folder, you need to rotate the pictures entitled *Fire_01* and *Night_01*. Because you don't want to apply this correction to all images, select only certain pictures, and then rotate them.

1 In the image preview on the right, click the picture you want to rotate. In this case, the file *Fire_01.tif* is selected.

Re-exposure of fire_01
1.885.872 bytes
970x648x24b tiff
25.01.2002 12:03

Rotating several pictures

Do you want to rotate several pictures by the same number of degrees? Select the pictures you want to rotate by clicking first on one and then pressing the [Ctrl] key while clicking the rest of the pictures in random order.

2. Optimizing images fast and easy

2 Go to *Tools/Rotate*. A dialog box opens in which you can determine the direction to rotate the picture. In this case, the third button in the *Apply the same adjustment to all images* area has been selected. The images referred to here are all the images you have selected, not all the images in the folder. The picture is rotated clockwise by 90°. Confirm your choice to apply the command; then exit the status report by clicking *Close*.

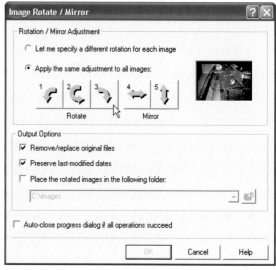

Beware of quality loss: Rotate pictures only once

Be aware that every pixel needs to be computed anew each time you rotate a picture. This procedure results in a certain quality loss. This is particularly true of compressed file formats like JPG. Therefore, whenever possible, rotate pictures into the right position only once. To keep the loss of details to a minimum, work with a loss-free format such as TIF, BMP, PSD, or RAW when rotating.

Optimizing the contrast of all pictures at once

The contrast correction feature in ACDSee is especially convenient, for it can be automatically applied to all pictures within a folder. This way, you can correct all pictures without having to confirm the correction of every single one. You also have the option of viewing every change in contrast and of confirming it or skipping the current picture. In the example, ACDSee awaits confirmation for each picture.

> **A high contrast might mean detail loss**
>
> When editing pictures, you might be inclined to create especially high contrasts or to sharpen the image considerably. Most people intuitively go with the idea that "more is better". However, be aware that heightening the contrast (that is pushing the gray tones towards black and white) can cause data loss. If you increase the contrast too much to bring out the blues in the picture, slight shapes in the sky can be lost, for instance. The effect corresponds in analog photography to using harsh contrasts. (By the way, the term "gradation curve" also comes from using contrast grades.) – the harsher the contrast, the fewer the gray tones.

1 Click one of the thumbnails in the list on the right to make sure you are in the thumbnail area. From the *Edit* menu, choose the *Select All* command.

2 After you have selected all the pictures, go to *Tools/Exposure*.

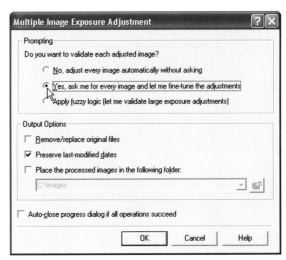

3 Because you want to make use of confirmation prompts in this project, enable the option *Yes, ask me for every image and let me fine-tune the adjustment*. In this dialog box, you can also decide whether you want to save the edited images as copies or whether you want to overwrite the originals. Enable the option *Preserve last-modified dates*. This ensures that a copy of the picture is saved with the prefix *Re-exposure of*.

> **Saving original data**
>
> It usually makes sense to save the original pictures and work with copies. This way, you ensure that you can return to the old version if you don't like your correction. Be aware, however, that only loss-free formats like TIF, BMP, PSD, or RAW should be saved repeatedly. JPG compressed files lose details with every successive save.

4 Confirm your choice in the dialog box. ACDSee now shows you the first picture and the suggested corrections. If you are happy with the correction, click *Yes*; if you want to make changes, however, click the button with the double arrow located at the right of *Help*.

5 The dialog box is expanded by three sliders for correcting the tonal value. Here, you can determine the darkest and lightest areas of the picture and change the mid-tones by moving the gamma slider.

6 Because the picture in the example had too few dark tonal values, the *Black* slider has been pushed up by about a third, so that the dark grays have become black. The *Gamma* slider has also been lowered to make the mid-tones appear fuller. If you like the correction, click *Yes*.

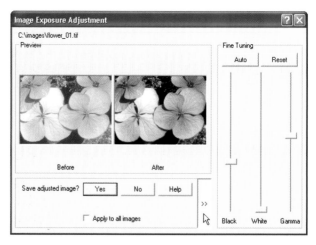

The contrast correction settings: Black, white, and gamma

If a picture appears to lack contrast, it is because the picture isn't using the full color spectrum from white (0%) to black (100%). The color gamut runs only from 10 to 85%, for instance. During automatic contrast corrections, ACDSee spreads the distribution of the tonal values over the whole spectrum.

Use the Black, White, and Gamma sliders to determine manually how the tonal values are distributed in the picture. Imagine that the darkest pixel in your picture has a value of 90% black. In this case, you aren't using the whole color spectrum from 0% to 100%. Move the Black slider upwards by 10% to compute the distribution of tonal values anew. Black now starts at 100%, and you are using all the tonal values available in the color spectrum. The same goes for the White slider. If your picture contains only gray pixels but no white ones, you can correct this with the White slider. Move the slider upwards until the brightest pixel is clearly white. These actions heighten the contrast of the picture. With the Gamma slider, you can correct the mid-tones, that is the gray values from 40 to 60%. If the mid-tones of a picture are too dark, shift the Gamma slider upwards.

7 Proceed in this way with all the pictures. Evaluate each picture separately, and either confirm the proposed corrections or manually optimize the settings; then click *Yes*. All pictures in our sample folder now have perfect contrast. However, some missing corrections are described in the following chapters.

Automatic image editing with XN View

XN View is an image viewer that supports all the usual formats and creates a thumbnail preview. In addition, XN View gives you the possibility of creating slide shows and of editing your images. You can apply filter effects and automate many tasks with the batch function. XN View is freeware and can be downloaded from the following Internet address: *http://www.xnview.com*

Cropping pictures easily and rapidly

With snapshots especially, you often find that the image area is not quite ideal. Not long ago, you needed a special image editing program to determine the optimal image area after taking the picture. However, ACDSee relieves you of performing this task.

The previous corrections could all be made in the regular view; however, for detail corrections, you must start the editor.

1 Select the picture you want to crop by clicking it, and then go to *Tools/Open in Editor*.

Protect yourself against pixel waste: Optimize the image area while photographing, if possible.

You can always select the image area after you take the picture, but this procedure has a disadvantage: Pixels that could have been used to render details more accurately are being wasted because they are cut away. For this reason, pay as much attention as possible to framing your image right while photographing.

2 In the example, the picture sunset_01 must be cropped to eliminate the black border. In the editor, you can find the *Crop* tool in the toolbar at the top. Click it to enable it.

Crop

3 With this tool, create a frame around the area you want to keep by clicking in the upper corner of the picture and dragging the mouse to the lower-right corner, making sure to press the mouse button simultaneously. You can see the selection frame when you let go of the mouse button.

4 Adjust the selection frame by pulling on the little boxes until the area you want to keep is framed in perfectly. Everything inside the selection frame is kept after the cropping.

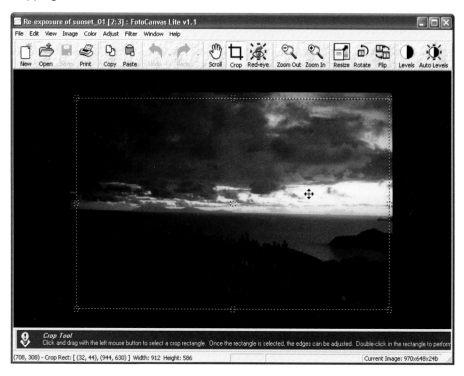

Cropping pictures to size

With ACDSee, you can crop pictures to a certain size as well. In the editor, go to *Image/Canvas Size*. In the dialog box, enter the desired width and height in pixels. Click *OK*, and the picture is cropped to the specified size (the image area is measured uniformly from the center of the image).

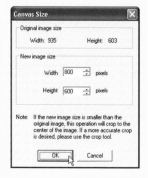

5 Double-click inside the selection frame to get rid of the undesired part of the image. If you like the new image area, close the editor by going to *File/Exit*. ACDSee then asks you if you want to save the file. Confirm the safety query to return to the regular ACDSee view.

Cropping in Paint Shop Pro

In Paint Shop Pro, the *Crop* tool comes with even more conveniences. In the *Tool Options* palette, you can establish the coordinates for the corners of the selection frame, which allows you to crop the picture precisely. This option frees you from having to measure the area you want to keep from the center, as in ACDSee.

When you crop pictures with the methods described, the pixels are not computed anew but removed uniformly from around the image area you want to keep. The image area suffers no loss in quality, and you can crop your pictures as many times as you want, until you are happy with the image. Only when you blow up the picture do the pixels shift, which makes the picture less sharp.

Optimizing the colors

Problematic lighting conditions can cause color casts in your pictures. If the color cast is uniformly distributed throughout the picture, you don't have to select a certain part of the picture and can correct the colors in ACDSee in a few steps. For more minute corrections (like the one described in the last section of this chapter), you need a more complex software like Paint Shop Pro. The color correction in ACDSee is usually all you need, however.

Color correction in practice

When you are correcting the colors of a picture, bear in mind that the human eye (actually, the brain) gets used to color casts and compensates for them. For this reason, it makes sense to take a break now and then before you proceed with complex color corrections. It might also happen that you overedit the colors and would like to return to an older version, so save any interim versions of the picture.

Correcting color casts with the color balance feature

The correction described here functions in other programs under the name *Color balance*. It is based on the RGB color system, that is the system with which monitors, digital cameras, scanners, TVs and video projectors work. RGB is an additive color system, which means that if you add all colors together you obtain white. Color casts are basically compensated by adding the complementary color (that is the color that lies across the cast color on the color wheel).

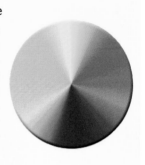

1 From your collection, open a picture that has an even color cast. From the sample folder, the image tree_01.tif has been selected. It shows a strong green cast, which you learn how to remove in the next steps.

2 Click the desired picture and go to *Tools/Open in Editor*.

3 To correct the color cast, use the command *Adjust/Red/Green/Blue*. If your picture, too, has a green cast, move the *Green* slider to the left.

4 Underneath the slider, you can see the effect of your editing by comparing the before and after preview images. The small images might be hard to evaluate, so click *Proof* to see a preview of the correction in the original picture.

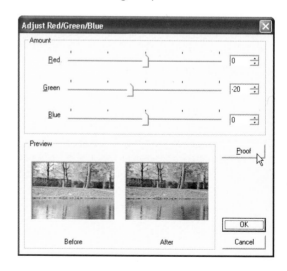

2. Optimizing images fast and easy

5 If you're not yet happy with the correction, try out different positions for the slider and watch the effect on the picture. When you have removed the color cast, confirm the dialog box.

6 If the correction in ACDSee doesn't remove the color cast, go to the last section in this chapter where the detail correction in Paint Shop Pro is described.

The RGB mode

RGB - Red, Green, Blue - is the system of radiant colors. In this system, the colors are obtained by addition; a combination of all the colors results in white. The colors on the monitor are represented with this system. All graphics intended for the Internet are also created in this color mode.

The CMYK mode

The CMYK system of pigments consists of cyan, magenta, yellow and contrast (black). Unlike the RGB mode, the colors in this system are obtained by subtraction, because all colors combined result in black. This mode is used for all printed material and does not apply to Web design.

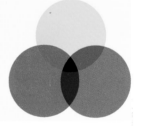

How many colors does your picture have?

The term bit is an abbreviation for "binary digit". It is the smallest unit of data in a computer. The number of colors you can have is 2n, where "n" is the bit depth of your picture. Line drawings with a color depth of 1 bit have 2^1 colors, that is they can be represented in two colors. If you have a color depth of 8 bit, you can already have 2^8 or 256 colors. In the true color mode of 24 bit, you can represent 2^{24} = 16.7 million colors.

An overview of bit depths

1 bit, 2^1,
black and white

4 bit, 2^4,
16 shades of gray,
no dithering

4 bit, 2^4,
16 shades of gray,
dithering

8 bit, 2^8,
265 shades of gray

2. Optimizing images fast and easy

4 bit, 2^4,
16 colors,
no dithering

4 bit, 2^4,
16 colors,
dithering

8 bit, 2^8,
256 colors

24 bit, 2^{24},
16.7 million colors

Chili for your pictures: Simple and perfect image sharpening

One of the most usual corrections during digital editing is the sharpening of the image. Pixel images lose sharpness not only when they are taken but also when you change the resolution and image size or when you rotate them. Even if you are using a high-quality camera, you might find it necessary to sharpen the image after taking the picture.

Sharpening in ACDSee

ACDSee offers you an automatic sharpening filter that you can adjust and which can be applied uniformly to the entire picture. This filter works well for pictures that need only a little sharpening, which is enough in most cases. For more complex corrections, use Paint Shop Pro, for there you can adjust the sharpness more precisely.

Print versus Web

Please bear in mind that any kind of sharpening appears stronger on the monitor than in print. All printing processes lead to a certain loss in sharpness. You should adjust the sharpening depending on whether you want to use your pictures for printed media or on-screen.

1 In the regular image preview, click the picture you want to edit and select *Tools/Open in Editor* once again.

2 You can monitor the sharpness of a picture on-screen only when the view is at 100%. Any other scaling factor produces a certain blurring. To view the picture at 100%, select the command *View/Actual Size*.

3 In the editor menu bar, go to *Filter/Sharpen*. Here you can adjust the sharpness on a scale from 0 to 100. The ideal setting depends on the subject of your picture. Try out a value and click *Proof* to view the result.

4 The picture flower_02 has a sharpness value of 100. If you are happy with the degree of sharpness, click *OK*.

2. Optimizing images fast and easy

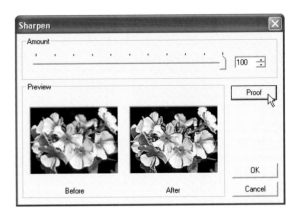

5 If you need to sharpen the picture some more, return to *Filter/Sharpen*.

6 When you are done sharpening the picture, confirm the dialog box and close the editor to return to the regular ACDSee view.

Over-sharpening produces irregularities in the picture

The impression of sharpness is produced by heightening the contrast between neighboring pixels. If you sharpen the image too much, some pixels might become oversaturated, and the image might appear grainy.

Sharpening in Paint Shop Pro

Not every picture can be optimized with a simple sharpen filter; sometimes you need to sharpen only certain areas. Paint Shop Pro comes with numerous sharpen filters that can be tailored to the individual requirements for your photograph. Examples of these filters are *Edge/Enhance* and *Unsharp Mask*. The Unsharp Mask filter belongs to the most important sharpen filters, because it analyzes the picture and sharpens only certain areas.

Unsharp Mask

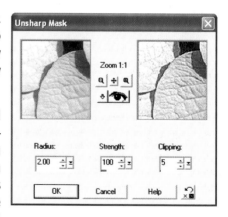

Most programs come with *the Unsharp Mask* filter. What makes this function so attractive are the *Clipping* and *Radius* options. To use these functions correctly, you should know how they work. During unsharp masking, the contrast between neighboring pixels that have different brightness values is additionally increased. The *Radius* option allows you to determine how many pixels to apply the effect to within the area to be sharpened. The higher the value, the more pixels that are affected by the sharpening. You can choose a value between 0.1 and 100 pixels, but in practice, values of up to 10 pixels work best. Larger values lead to the over-saturation of individual pixels. Basically, the higher the resolution of the image, the larger the radius might be. If you are creating pictures for use on the Internet – which usually have a resolution of 72 dpi – the radius should not be bigger than about 3 pixels.

The *Clipping* value determines how high the contrast between neighboring pixels must be in order for them to be sharpened. The higher the clipping value, the lower the degree of sharpening. A low clipping value reinforces irregularities in the picture (like noise). Such pictures are best sharpened a number of times using a higher clipping value.

1 Start Paint Shop Pro and open the picture of your choice with the command *File/Open*. Here, too, it is important to choose a 100% or 1:1 view. To do so, select the command *View/Normal Viewing (1:1)*. This command is only available if your picture is not already in this view.

2 Go to *Effects/Sharpen/Unsharp Mask*. Click the button with the stylized eye to preview the settings. Click the small arrow next to the eye icon to display the preview on the entire screen.

3 The settings in this dialog box depend on the subject of your picture, so try different values. The example demonstrates a radius of 2 pixels, a strength of 100, and a clipping of 0. A clipping value of 0 allows the contrast of all neighboring pixels to be heightened, independent of their original contrast.

2. Optimizing images fast and easy

Rescuing extremely blurred images

Unfortunately, it often happens that an attractive subject is so blurred that even a sharpen filter cannot obtain better picture quality. In such cases, you can save the picture by applying a texturing effect to it, for instance. In this example, the command *Effects/Texture Effects/Fine Leather* in Paint Shop Pro was applied with the settings *Blur 0, Number of furrows 50, Length of furrows 4* and *Transparency 248*.

Adjusting the image sharpness with the aperture size

Most digital cameras have two or three different aperture settings. The setting of the aperture determines the depth of field. At first, it might be somewhat confusing that a small f-stop number means a large aperture size, letting in a lot of light. The depth of field and sharpness are then reduced. The f-stop number determines the aperture size. Usual f-stop values are: 1.4, 2.0, 2.8, 4.0, 5.6, 8, 11, 16, 22. The highest value, 22, stands for the smallest aperture size and conversely – the smallest value, 1.4, stands for the largest aperture size. Please bear in mind that with a small aperture size (that is, a large f-stop number) you need a long exposure time, which can lead to blurring. For long exposure times, make sure you are holding the camera steady, using a tripod or another solid base.

Note

Shutter speed

Next to the aperture size, the shutter speed is the most important factor in controlling the exposure. The aperture size determines the quantity of light falling in, the shutter speed determines the exposure time. If your digital camera allows you to adjust the shutter speed manually, use it to actively design your picture. If you are photographing something in movement but want your picture to be as sharp as possible, use a short exposure time. If, on the other hand, you want to use motion blur as an effect, use a longer exposure time. If you want to have the effect of motion blur but your camera doesn't allow you to control the shutter speed, use the *Motion Blur* filter by going to *Effects/Blur/Motion Blur*. A camera with automatic shutter speed adjustment measures the quantity of light falling in and turns off the CCD when it has received enough light.

Determining the image size

Digital images are bitmaps, that is, pictures that are composed of individual pixels. The total number of pixels gives you the size of the image, depending on the resolution. For instance, if the width of a picture has a total of 600 pixels and the resolution is 100 dpi, your picture is 6 inches wide.

The image size dialog box in ACDSee is not useful, for you only have the option of changing the total number of pixels. In Paint Shop Pro, you can choose between pixel size and actual print size.

Note

Ppi and dpi

The abbreviations ppi (pixel per inch) and dpi (dots per inch) basically describe the same thing, that is, the density of data measured in pixels over a distance of one inch. The more pixels per inch, the higher the resolution. Some programs use the term ppi, some dpi, but don't let that confuse you.

In the following steps, you want to solve this problem: a picture loaded from the digital camera has a total number of 1200 × 870 pixels at a resolution of 72 dpi. You want to print the picture on an inkjet printer at a resolution of 200 dpi and a width of 5 inches.

2. Optimizing images fast and easy

1 Start Paint Shop Pro, open a picture, and select *Image/Resize*.

2 At the top of the dialog box, you can see the *Pixel size*; in the example, that's 1200 × 870 pixels.

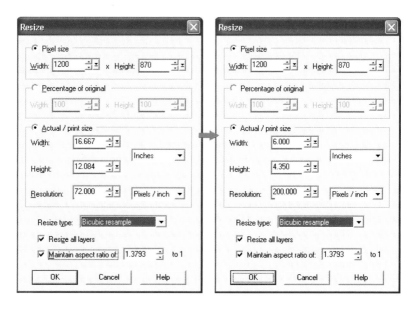

3 Enable the option *Actual/print size*. At this point, the picture still has a resolution of 72 dpi. If you printed it out at this resolution, you would obtain a picture of 16.7 × 12 inches.

4 Because a resolution of 72 dpi is too low for a printout – the image appears pixelated –recompute it to 200 dpi. This new distribution of the pixels gives you a new image width. Enter a value of 200 dpi in the *Resolution* field.

5 You must select the resize type *Bicubic resample* in the lower half of the dialog box, and enable the options *Resize all layers* and *Maintain aspect ratio of*. If you don't enable the latter option, the image is disproportionately distorted.

6 Now read the new *Width*. You see that the new distribution of pixels results in a width of 6 inches. Because the picture should be only 5 inches wide, enter the value *5 Inches* in the *Width* field. Confirm the dialog box with *OK*, and the superfluous pixels are removed.

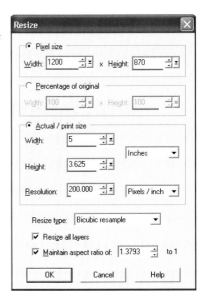

Enlarging and shrinking images

When you are scaling an image – that is, enlarging or shrinking it – you need to either add new pixels to the image or remove existing ones. This is made possible by interpolation. The selected resize type determines how the pixels should be re-computed. Paint Shop Pro gives you four different interpolation methods: *Smart size, Bilinear resample, Bicubic resample*, and *Pixel resize*.

During the *Smart size* procedure, Paint Shop Pro analyzes your picture and uses the method most suited to it.

Bicubic resample is the best resizing method for most pictures. It necessitates the longest computation, but it also treats your pictures gently. With this method, you obtain the highest-quality photographs, so it makes sense to define it as your default method.

The *Bilinear resample* method is similar to *Bicubic resample* but achieves only medium quality. This method works by computing averages for neighboring pixels.

Pixel resize is the fastest interpolation method. It uses no anti-aliasing – that is, it doesn't smooth out any edges. With this method you might save computation time, but your pictures show little zigzags instead of rounded corners. This method is best used when you are scaling pictures with horizontal and vertical lines.

The pattern on the left was scaled using the pixel resize interpolation method. For the picture on the right, the bicubic resample method was used. The effects illustrate how differently the two methods function from each other.

Picture formats at optimum resolution

For the ideal inkjet printout, you need a resolution of 200 dpi. For a professional offset print, you need a resolution of 300 dpi. In the following table, you can find out which picture formats you can obtain at an optimum resolution.

Mega-pixels	Optimum printout format for an inkjet printer (200 dpi resolution) in inches	Picture size in pixels	Data amount
1	6.4 × 4.8	1280 × 960	about 3.5 MB
2	9 × 6	1800 × 1200	about 6 MB
3	10 × 7.5	2000 × 1500	about 8.5 MB
4	11.4 × 8.5	2272 × 1704	about 11 MB
5	12.8 × 9.6	2560 × 1920	about 14 MB

Enlarge pictures only in an emergency

Enlarging pictures always results in quality loss, because your image-editing program needs to compute additional pixels for the image. Whenever possible, avoid enlargements of over 130%. Your program tries to insert pixels as inconspicuously as possible, but unfortunately, that is only possible at the expense of quality. The picture loses sharpness and brilliancy. The program S Spline 2.0 promises gentler enlargement. It is available at *http://www.shortcut.nl*

The image resolution

The image resolution gives you the total number of pixels in the picture. The resolution is given in dpi (dots per inch) or ppi (pixel per inch), and is the resolution at which you scanned or photographed your picture. The higher the resolution, the higher the quality and richer the detail of the picture displayed. If you print out a picture with a low resolution, notice that the printout looks pixelated.

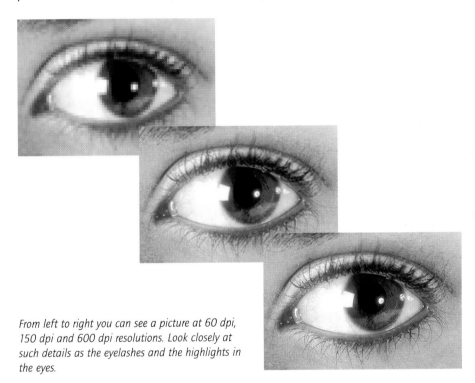

From left to right you can see a picture at 60 dpi, 150 dpi and 600 dpi resolutions. Look closely at such details as the eyelashes and the highlights in the eyes.

Note

After scaling, always sharpen the picture somewhat

Scaling pictures always results in a loss in quality, which is higher for images at high resolutions than for those at lower ones. For this reason, it is a good idea to sharpen the image afterwards by going to *Effects/Sharpen/Unsharp Mask*.

The sky is gray and dull

It often happens that the sky stands out negatively in an otherwise attractive picture, because it is gray and lacks contrast. Paint Shop Pro can help you in such a case. Select the sky with the help of the *Magic Wand* and correct it independently from the rest of the photograph.

1 Open an image file for which you want to refresh the sky. Enable the *Magic Wand*. It is the eighth tool from the top in the toolbar.

The Magic Wand

The *Magic Wand* selects pixels of similar tonal value that form a limit of some kind. In the *Tool options* palette, define the tolerance. The tolerance determines how large the difference between the tonal values of neighboring pixels might be for the pixels to be selected.

2 Next, adjust the *Magic Wand* options. To do so, open the *Tool options* palette. Select *View/Toolbars*, which gives you the palette selection. Check the box next to *Tool Options Palette* and click *OK*. The style palette appears.

3 Enter a value for the tolerance. For our example, a tolerance value of 50 works well, but what works depends on the subject of your picture, and you must try out different values to find the ideal one for your image.

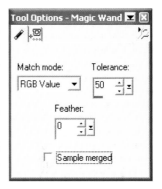

4 Now click the sky. Paint Shop Pro selects the same tonal values. If large differences in contrast appear in your picture, the whole sky might not be selected at once. Press and hold the (Shift) key (notice a small plus sign next to the magic wand) and click in the areas you also want to select. Paint Shop Pro adds the new areas to the existing selection.

5 Repeat this procedure until the whole sky is selected. Now you can correct the tonal value.

6 Go to *Colors/Adjust/Red/Green/Blue*. In this dialog box, you can add different amounts of color in percents. In the example, a medium blue with the values

2. Optimizing images fast and easy

Red -20%, Green 0% and *Blue +40%* has been created. Find the ideal settings for your subject by trying out different values and watching the image preview. When you're done, confirm the dialog box.

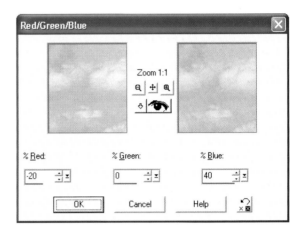

7 In addition to the color correction, you also want to heighten the contrast of the cloudy sky. Go to *Colors/Adjust/Brightness/Contrast*. You have increased the contrast by 10%. Confirm the dialog box.

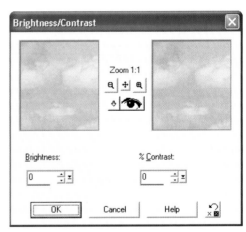

8 Now deselect the sky by going to *Selections/Select None*.

2. Optimizing images fast and easy

Easy and fast effects

ACDSee and Paint Shop Pro feature a wide range of effect filters. Use these filters to add special touches to your digital photographs. Combining multiple filters can often create particularly appealing results. In this chapter, you add the charming characteristics usually found in older photographs to your images. You use color effects and as well as border and text effects.

Turning the new into the old – Black-and-white or sepia images

Use ACDSee to turn your photographs into sepia-toned images with one click of the mouse. In case you want to cast your photos in a color other than light brown, use the *Colorize* function. Use the *Hue* and *Saturation* controls to select the color and its intensity.

3. Easy and fast effects

Note

Choosing the appropriate color mode

It is possible to apply a sepia tint to both black-and-white images and color photos. It is important to work in Truecolor mode because the *Sepia* filter is not available in other modes. Change the mode by selecting *Color* in the ACDSee editor.

1 Select an image in the ACDSee preview and select *Tools/Open in Editor* from the menu bar.

2 Select *Filter/Sepia* to change the image's coloration into duotone. The result is a soft brown tint.

3 If you would like to emphasize the color a little more, as in the example, go to *Adjust/Hue/Saturation/Lightness*.

4 If you move only the *Saturation* slider to the right, the tonal value doesn't change, only the saturation level increases (in the example, we increased the saturation level by *50*).

Note

What is saturation?

The level of saturation is a measure of the purity of a color on a scale from grey to full color.

5 If you want to apply another color to change the overall tint of your image, also adjust the *Hue* slider. At around *50*, the picture is tinted with blue, which creates a more mystical atmosphere for your image than the warm brown tone.

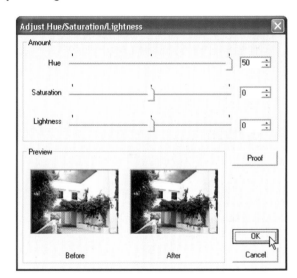

Fascinating color effects

To create truly surreal color effects in ACDSee, work with the same dialog box you used before. This type of effect is easily created and adds a special atmosphere to your image. If you move the *Hue* slider without applying the sepia effect first, all colors are shifted on the color wheel by the same value.

3. Easy and fast effects

1 Open the image in the ACDSee editor.

2 Select *Adjust/Hue/Saturation/Lightness*. Move the *Hue* slider and look at the preview window. Notice that all colors are changing.

Creating the same effect in Paint Shop Pro

In Paint Shop Pro, this dialog box can be found under *Colors/Adjust/ Hue/Saturation/Lightness*. You can create the same effects as in ACDSee. In addition, as you change the colors, monitor the changes in the color wheels shown in the dialog box. The outer circle shows the original color, the middle circle shows the level of saturation and the inner circle represents the new color. In the example, red turns into cyan and green turns into purple.

Using filters separately and in combination

Review the next table for examples of fascinating effects available in ACDSee and Paint Shop Pro. All these filters are located in the *Filter* (ACDSee) and *Effects* (Paint Shop Pro) menus respectively. Some filters are particularly interesting when used in combination with others. The examples show you only the tip of the iceberg of creations that can be achieved with your software. Use your imagination!

Effects in ACDSee

Emboss

Azimuth 45
Elevation 45
Weight 3

Edge Detect

3. Easy and fast effects

Oil Paint

Brush Width 3
Variance 125
Vibrance 1

Negative

Effects in Paint Shop Pro

Artistic Effects/Aged Newspaper

Amount to age 75

Artistic Effects/Brush Strokes

Length 10
Density 25
Bristles160
Width 5
Opacity 50
Softness 10

Try different settings with this particular filter, because the results can vary drastically.

3. Easy and fast effects

Artistic Effects/Charcoal

Detail 100
Opacity 50

Artistic Effects/Chrome

Flaws 2
Brightness 0
Color Blue

In addition, the contrast correction *Colors/Histogram Functions/Equalize* were applied.

Artistic Effects/Enamel

Blur
Detail
Density

Use this filter for sparse landscapes. The results are amazing!

Geometric Effects/Circle

Choose from a wide variety of distortions in the *Geometric Effects* menu.

3. Easy and fast effects

Illumination Effects/Lights

This filter is incredibly flexible. Create different spotlights, each with its own individual properties. The *Presets* drop-down menu contains a number of interesting predefined spot effects.

Texture Effects/Polished Stone

Texture Effects/Sculpture

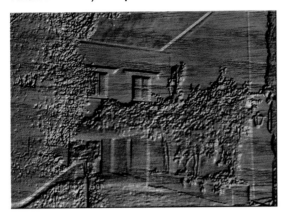

This filters is incredibly versatile. For example, it allows you to create copperplate etchings. In this image, the *Mahogany* filter was selected from the *Presets* drop-down menu.

Texture Effects/Texture

This filter is a portal to countless other filters. The example demonstrates using the *Plastic wrinkles* preset.

3. Easy and fast effects

Texture Effects/Weave

Solarizing dull images

Did you capture an interesting object on camera, but gray skies and rain made the image's colors appear pale and lacking in contrast? Try solarizing the image. (This might work for some images but not all.) Sometimes solarizing creates a true piece of art; other times the result does not look good at all.

Image composition

While chaos can sometimes be used as a stylistic device, with most images you should normally try to avoid it. As the human eye always looks for ordered structures, create a coherent image by focusing on a particular segment in your image or by creating a certain rhythm, which can consist of a sequence of rocks, steps or connecting arches, for instance.

1 Find an image that has little contrast and open it in Paint Shop Pro. Images of barren landscapes with overcast skies look particularly pretty after solarization. You will be surprised!

2 Select *Colors/Solarize*. A *Threshold* of *128 has been selected*. Try using other values if necessary; then click *OK*.

3 The result might look somewhat dull at first. Select *Colors/Histogram Functions/Equalize* to increase the contrast and lighten the colors.

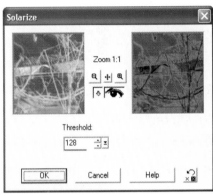

3. Easy and fast effects

The use of solarization in classic photography

The solarization effect has its roots in classic analog photography. There, it is called pseudo-solarization. The effect is created through a complex procedure. As a first step, the image is exposed normally. Then, the film is developed in a bath that needs to remain entirely motionless. After half the development time has passed, the room light is switched on briefly. This causes the lighter sections of the image to be exposed and developed as well. An almost white line appears at the transition points between light and dark segments, increasing the contrast. Through contact printing you can then obtain a positive defamiliarization.

Walking on the edge – Effects for the image borders

Paint Shop Pro has a Wizard that helps with the creation of frames for your images and does most of the work for you. A frame can be placed inside the current image borders, hiding some of the outer segments of the image. Alternatively, use the Wizard to increase the canvas area and place a frame around the image, keeping the entire picture intact. That Paint Shop Pro creates each frame on a separate layer is particularly useful. This way you can change the filters or colors and apply the changes only to the frame, without altering the image.

1 Go to *Image/Picture Frame* and select *Navy Metallic* from the drop-down menu; then click *Next*.

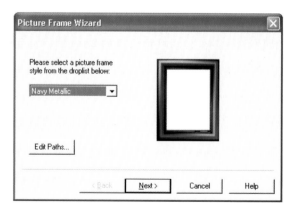

2 In the subsequent dialog box, specify whether the frame should be inside the image or outside it. In the example, you apply the *Twirl* filter, so it is important to select the *Frame inside of the image* option. Click *Done.*

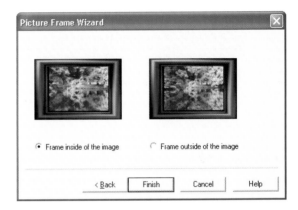

3. Easy and fast effects

3 The frame is now created, and you are going to customize it further. The colors should match the content of the image. Activate the *Layer Palette* by right-clicking into an empty area (for instance, an empty area inside the standard toolbar). This opens a pop-up menu. Select the *Layer Palette* option by clicking it. The *Layer Palette* opens.

4 By default, the palette opens when you hold your mouse over it. To stop this behavior, click the black arrow in the top right corner. This button is called *Lock window open*: The palette now remains open.

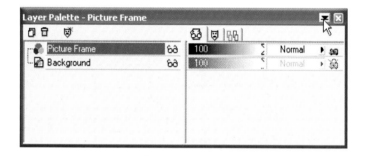

5 Go to *Colors/Adjust/Hue/Saturation/Lightness* and activate the preview icon (depicting an eye). Move the sliders until the color of the frame matches the overall colors of your image.

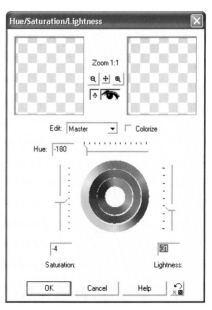

6 The color of the frame has been adjusted, but you want to add a little extra by using the *Twirl* filter. Go to *Effects/Geometric Effects/Twirl*. Experiment with different values. The example shows a *Degrees* value of 460°.

Photographing reflections

Basically, you can use any digital camera to photograph reflections. When you do so, create as large a contrast as possible. This works best if the reflective surface (for example, a body of water) is covered by shade, while the reflected objects (for example trees or houses) are in full sunlight.

Expressive: Inserting text into your image

The text-editing functions of all text-editing programs are becoming more and more extensive and increasingly user friendly. Until you convert the text to a raster layer (that is, change it from vectors to pixels), you can edit it any way you want. You can change both the text itself and its formatting. In this chapter, you work with the *Layer Palette*, using different blend modes that help you insert your text into the image as if it were partially transparent.

1 Open any image to which you want to add a headline in Paint Shop Pro. Enable the *Text* tool (it is the fourth tool from the bottom in the toolbar and looks like an A).

2 Click inside your image to open the text editor. Type in the desired text. If you want to break it up into different lines, hit Return to start each new line.

3 After you have composed your text, press Ctrl+A. This action selects the entire text, which you can now format.

Formatting text in Paint Shop Pro

In the text editor of Paint Shop Pro, you can even select individual letters with the mouse and apply different formats to each.

4 In the example, the font *Arial Black* has been selected from the *Name* list box. For the text effects you use, select a font that is as bold as possible, so the color combination is easily visible. From the *Size* list box, select a font size. Adapt the line spacing to your font size. Paint Shop Pro shows you any changes to the text in the preview window as they happen. In the *Styles* category, you can change the *Stroke* and *Fill* colors. Click the *Fill* field.

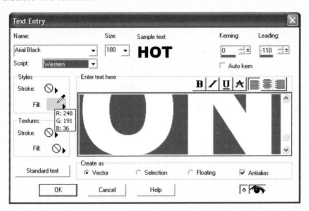

Smoothing out the text

At the bottom of the *Text Entry* dialog window, locate a check box marked *Antialias*. As a rule, it makes sense to enable this option. Antialising is a procedure by which the letter edges are blended into the background. The outer-most pixels are blurred, so the little jagged edges that are characteristic of programs using pixels are hidden. Anti-aliasing is bothersome only if you have a small font size and a low image resolution; in that case, you should disable the function.

5 After you click the color field, the *Color* dialog box opens. With the mouse, select a color (for example, from the *Basic colors* palette). When you're done, confirm both dialog boxes.

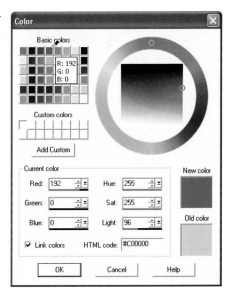

3. Easy and fast effects

6 The text is now inserted into your picture, but you still need to position it. Enable the *Mover* tool (the fifth tool from the top in the toolbar). Click the text and move it to the desired position while pressing the mouse button.

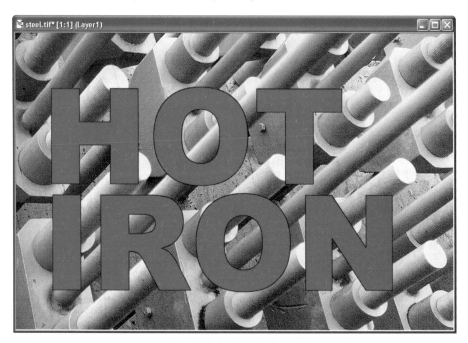

7 Make sure the *Layer Palette* is open. (If not, open it by right-clicking another palette and selecting the *Layer Palette* entry from the drop-down menu.) At this moment, the text lies on top of the image, covering the latter partially. This is the *Normal* layer blend mode, where the upper layer lies on top of the bottom layer, covering it. You want to use another layer blend mode, however, where the layer blending creates interesting color effects.

8 Make sure you are in the upper layer. You recognize the active layer by the blue highlighting. If you are unsure, click the *Layer1* entry in the *Layer Palette*. In the *Layer Blend Mode* field, you can see that the *Normal* mode is still selected. Select the *Overlay* entry from the drop-down menu and look at the image to see the changes. The layers are overlaying each other, which allows the colors to mix. Try different modes for a taste of the different possibilities.

Post-editing text

If you want to make changes to the text, enable the *Text* tool and click the text. The text editor opens once again, and you can make any changes you like.

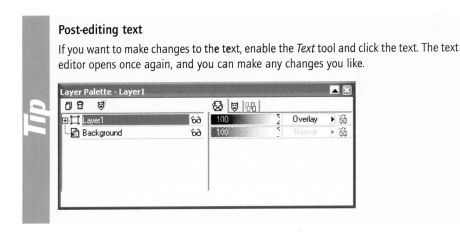

9 Be aware that images containing several layers cannot be saved as TIF or JPG files. You can save them in the layer-enabled PSP format, however. If you don't want to make any more changes to the text, you can also merge the layers. To do so, select the command *Layers/Merge/Merge all (Flatten)*.

3. Easy and fast effects

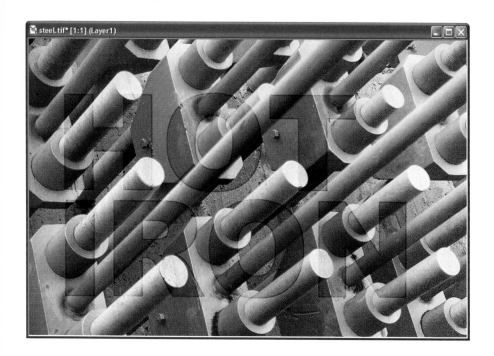

White balance

Every light source influences color differently. This influence is called color temperature. Images taken in incandescent light have a yellowish or reddish tint; neon light makes images appear green. For this reason, you need to do a white balance.

Your camera's automatic white balance determines the type of light source. But the automatic white balance has difficulties whenever your subject contains no white areas or whenever you have different light sources illuminating it.

For this reason, some cameras come with a manual white balance, so you can work it yourself.

Fooling the white balance

If your camera doesn't come with a manual white balance and the automatic one is encountering difficulties, try the following trick: before taking the picture, point your camera to a white object and press the shutter release half way to measure the light; then turn back to the subject you wanted to the original subject before the shutter releases entirely.

Try out a few white balance settings for each subject and compare them to find out which setting you like best. You might find that using the "wrong" white balance by design can result in attractive effects.

Camera filters

In this chapter, you have learned about numerous effects that you can apply directly in your image-editing program. However, you can also attach many filters to your digital camera, just as there are filters for the analog camera. The following table explains which filters are necessary and when you should use them.

- **Conversion filter**

  Conversion filters are supposed to convert artificial light to natural light. You can make this correction directly in your image-editing program (for example, in the *Color Balance* dialog box). This filter might even cause damage, for it interferes with the automatic white balance.

- **UV Haze filter**

  UV Haze and Infrared filters filter out light from these frequencies. This ensures an optimized color reproduction.

- **Neutral Density filter**

  This filter is useful when you want to capture motion blur, for instance. The Neutral Density filter blocks out some of the light and thus allows longer exposure times. However, you can obtain motion blur in Paint Shop Pro, as well as by going to *Effects/Blur/Motion Blur*.

3. Easy and fast effects

- ## Colored filters

  By combining different filters and color corrections, you can create innumerable other effects as well. This makes colored filters for your camera rather unnecessary.

- ## Special effect filters

  These filters are not suitable for digital cameras, because they have been conceived for objectives with larger appertures and longer focal lengths. In Paint Shop Pro, go to *Effects/Geometric Effects* for some of these special effects.

- ## Lens hood

  Lens hoods or shades are useful. They protect the photograph from contrast losses and unwanted reflections. If you are using a flash when you are taking the picture, take the hood off. It is important to use the right hood for your camera. Ask for advice on the exact lens hood you need for your camera.

Tip

Interesting filter links

At *http://www.imaging-resource.com* and *http://www.Nikon.com*, you can find extensive Web sites that you can browse for tips not only on digital cameras, but also on printing, scanning, and software applications.

Goodbye bunny eyes – and other simple retouching secrets

Retouching is one of the most fascinating options of digital photography and image editing. In this chapter, you work with a blur filter to add depth to an image; you also learn to restore the natural color of red eyes – caused by the unpopular flash effect. In sections 3 and 4 of this chapter, you create a panorama picture and retouch it by using the clone brush tool to remove disturbing objects from a picture.

Adding emphasis by using the blur effect

The image background can be an important creative medium to literally display the background with a person in the image. On the other hand, a background can greatly distract from the foreground. In this project, you blur the background in Paint Shop Pro to put emphasis on the person. You work with three layers of the same image. The layers are on top of each other – just like you would place three copies or prints of the same picture on top of each other. You remove the background from the top layer of the layer stack by using an eraser tool, and a blur filter is applied to the layer in the middle. The lowest layer acts as a safety layer in case accidentally erase some parts of the foreground.

4. Goodbye bunny eyes – and other simple retouching secrets

Three tips about depth of field

Depth of field describes the sharpness of objects in front and behind the object you are focusing on. Three factors are important in this connection: the lens aperture, the focal length of your lens, and the distance between the camera and the selected object.

Consider this basic rule regarding the *lens aperture*: The smaller the lens opening, the greater your depth of field. The same principle applies when a person squints his or her eyes to focus on something. At an f-stop of 22, you have the best chances of precisely capturing a lying person from tip to toe, if there's sufficient light. In terms of *focal length*, however, the following rule applies: The depth of field decreases with an increasing focal length. With a 28mm wide angle lens, the background is clearly in focus, whereas a 135mm lens lightly blurs the background. Consequently, additional emphasis is placed on the foreground.

When it comes to distance, use the following rule of thumb: The depth of field increases the greater the distance between lens and object.

1 Open a picture such as a portrait, for instance, in Paint Shop Pro. The image should contain a background that distracts from the foreground.

2 Select *File/Save As* and save a copy of the image. This copy acts as a backup copy as you might make mistakes when retouching an image.

3 The *Layer Palette* is particularly important in this project. Open it by right-clicking one of the palettes and selecting the entry *Layer Palette* from the pop-up menu.

4 The *Layer Palette* only contains one layer at this point – the Background layer. Duplicate this layer twice for this project. Select *Layers/Duplicate* and repeat this command. You then see three layers in the palette.

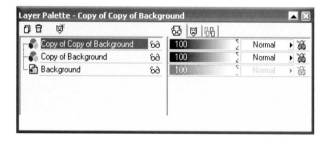

5 If you think the layer names *Copy of Copy of Background* and *Copy of Background*, which were assigned automatically, are too confusing, double-click the layer name in the layer palette. A dialog box opens in which you can rename the layers. You could call the top layer *Erase* and the middle layer *blur*, for instance. Logistic terms like these that refer to the particular editing function provide a better overview.

6 First, make the top layer *Erase* invisible by clicking the layer visibility toggle in the layer palette. Then activate the middle layer *blur* by clicking the layer name. The layer is then highlighted in blue.

7 Next, select *Effects/Blur/Gaussian blur*. Depending on how heavy the layer should be blurred, select a *Radius* of 30, for instance. This image layer is then entirely blurred. You have now finished the editing of this layer.

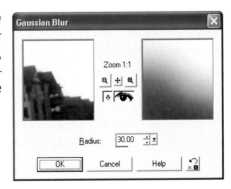

4. Goodbye bunny eyes – and other simple retouching secrets

8 Click the layer name of the *Erase* layer in the *Layer Palette*. The red X symbol that was displayed on top of the layer visibility toggle symbol has now disappeared, and the layer is visible and enabled again. You can now use the eraser to work on this layer.

9 Enable the *Eraser* tool. It is the 15th tool from the top in the toolbar. Set the *Tool Options* now. Open the *Tool Options* by right-clicking one of the palettes and selecting the corresponding entry from the pop-up menu.

10 Select the size of your brush tip. Refer to the illustration to choose the appropriate settings.

11 Click and hold your left mouse button. Erase the background of the *Erase* layer. It seems like you are blurring the background; however, you are actually removing the pixels of the top layer. Consequently, the blurred background on the middle layer *blur* appears.

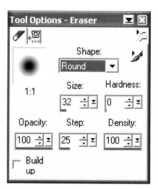

Erasing the background in many steps

While erasing the background, it is useful to release the mouse button once in a while; that is, it is recommended to erase the background in little steps. If you retouch large areas at once and you make a mistake, you must delete the entire last step – and consequently, the entire area you previously retouched is lost. Once you have successfully retouched an image section, release the mouse button; then continue retouching the image.

12 You should be particularly careful when working on the transition between background and foreground. You might want to use a smaller brush size or a higher zoom factor.

Setting the zoom factor

Most programs allow you to zoom in or zoom out of images by using the keyboard shortcut Ctrl+⊕ or Ctrl+⊖. Often, only the keys on the numeric keypad work for this shortcut, however. If your mouse contains a scroll wheel, you might want to try whether you can zoom in and out of images by using the scroll wheel. Many programs support this function.

13 If the entire background of the *Erase* layer has been removed and you don't want to do any further corrections, you can merge all of the layers by selecting *Layers/Merge/Merge all*.

The background layer is the backup layer

If you have accidentally removed an image section of the top layer and the Undo function in the Edit menu of Paint Shop Pro is not sufficient, you can always click the background layer, select *Layer/Duplicate,* and then drag the duplicate to the top of the layer palette. You can move a layer within the stack of layers by clicking it – approximately in the area of the layer name – pressing your mouse button, dragging it upwards, and then releasing the mouse button.

Normalizing red eyes

Fortunately, the unpopular red-eye effect does not occur as often as it used to as the newer cameras offer a new flash technology that prevents it. Once in a while, however, you might come across this problem. In this case, ACDSee and its automatic red eye correction come in handy.

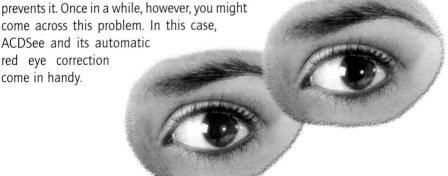

4. Goodbye bunny eyes – and other simple retouching secrets

1 Start ACDSee and go to a folder containing a red-eye picture. Click the image and select *Tools/Open in Editor*.

2 Enlarge the image by clicking Zoom until you find a size providing you with a good overview.

Zoom In

3 Click the *Red-eye Reduction* button; a bar allowing you to optimize the function opens afterwards.

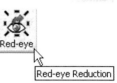

Red-eye

Red-eye Reduction

4 Select the eye color – which is *Brown* in this case. This way, ACDSee creates a clean transition between iris and pupil.

Tool Options - Red-eye

Amount: |——|—— 123 ÷   Eye Color: Brown ▼   ☑ Show Outline   Apply

5 Click and drag your mouse over the red pupil. ACDSee immediately reduces the red color. The standard value of *123* is not sufficient in this example, however. You must move the *Amount* slider to *246* to neutralize the red-eye effect.

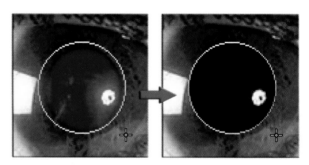

6 Once you are satisfied with your editing results, click *Apply*. Close the editor and save the image.

Creating your own panorama photos

Panorama photos are a particularly interesting challenge. With panorama photos, you can capture the entire panorama of fascinating landscapes. A number of tools that merge the individual shots are available now. Ulead has developed a convenient program called *Ulead COOL 360* that makes the merging of your panorama photos simple. You can go to the *Free Downloads* section of *http://www.ulead.com* to download a free trial version of the program.

Organizing shareware programs

If you are interested in shareware programs and you are downloading many programs, you could lose track of things.. It makes sense, therefore, to create a special directory (for example *C:\tools*) in which you can place a separate folder with a unique name for each individual program. If you save many programs without memorizing the location and name of the file, it might be difficult to find the file again because the file names of executable files are not always clear.

4. Goodbye bunny eyes – and other simple retouching secrets

Cool 360 allows you to correct perspective distortions, adjust differences in brightness and color and create smooth transitions between the individual panorama pictures. You can create entire 360° panorama pictures or merge only a few individual pictures. In the example, you assemble four single pictures.

1 Start Ulead COOL 360. You are greeted with a user-friendly start screen. At the top of the screen, you can find the main navigation menu with the three sections *Start, Adjust*, and *Finish*. In the Start section, you can see a selection menu on the right; here you can select the desired files. Click *New Project*.

2 In the dialog box that follows, you can specify whether you want to create a *Full 360° panorama*. Because you only want to merge four images, you must select the option *Wide angle image*. Assign a project name and select the directory the project should be saved in. In addition, you can enter a description of the project. Click *Next*.

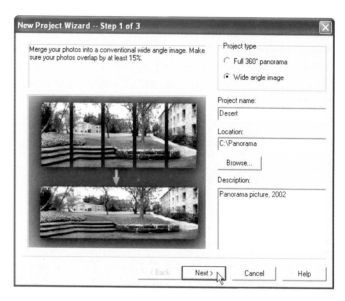

3 Search for your images in the next dialog box and select them by using your mouse. Confirm your selection by clicking *Add*. Your images are then displayed in the preview window. Click *Next* to open the next dialog window.

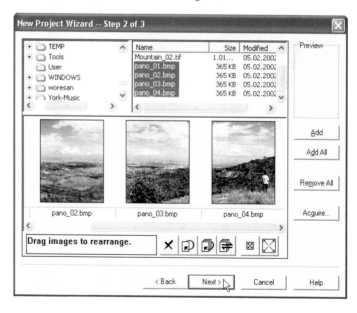

4. Goodbye bunny eyes – and other simple retouching secrets

4 You can already see a preview of the merged image. In the third dialog box it is important that you choose the *Camera lens* you took the individual pictures with. Selecting the correct lens prevents distortions. Ulead COOL 360 provides many of the current lens types in this list. If your camera is not in the list, select *Custom lens* in the main program, click *Settings* to download new lenses, and customize your lens parameters. Select 16mm for this example and click *Done*.

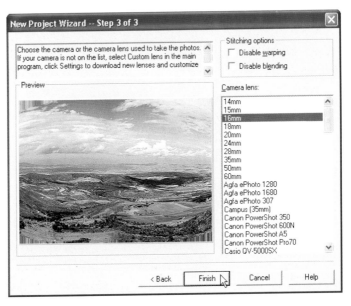

Paying attention to consistent exposure levels

The movement of clouds and perspective distortion are the difficulties you face when taking panorama pictures. If you are planning to shoot a 360° panorama picture, you should – if possible – pay attention to consistent exposure levels. Ideally, the sky should be evenly overcast as the clouds would consequently diffuse the sun light; your exposure levels would be consistent and distinct cloud outlines would not be a problem. If you prefer to take the pictures on a sunny day, you might encounter the problem of shooting against direct sunlight. A lens hood helps to achieve consistent exposure. At noon, when the sun has reached its highest point, you have the chance to avoid direct frontal sunlight. You could also wait until the sun is hiding behind a building or mountain.

5 You are now in the second section of the main navigation, the *Adjust* section. Your images are already placed side by side. You can click them individually and move them to make sure they were placed properly. This dialog box also allows you to rotate your images and apply perspective distortions. Select one image at a time and correct the position. To the right of the picture are sliders to correct *Hue, Saturation, Brightness*, and *Contrast* levels.

6 Scroll through the entire panorama picture by moving the small sphere below the panorama preview. Then click the individual images to edit them. COOL 360 creates smooth transitions between the individual images. Once you are satisfied with all of the settings, click the *Finish* entry in the navigation bar.

7 COOL 360 now merges the images, trims the top and bottom so that no step-wise irregularities occur between the individual images, and closes the circle in case you are working with full panorama pictures. If you want to see a preview of the entire

4. Goodbye bunny eyes – and other simple retouching secrets

panorama picture, click *Viewer*. If you created a full panorama picture, you can use the *Viewer* to navigate through the image just like you were using a flight simulator. Click the image and move it – you "fly" through the panorama image. Close the *Viewer* to save the image.

Tip

Tripods and panorama heads

It is not that easy to rotate your camera in regular intervals if you are holding it in your hands. If you are taking panorama pictures often, you might want to think about buying a tripod with a panorama head. You can find further interesting information about panorama hardware on the Website *http://www.kaidan.com*.

8 In the *Finish* section, you can decide whether you want to save your image or whether you want to send it to someone. You can send the image to a friend, for instance, by clicking the e-mail button. For this example, click *Save* and save your image in JPG format. If you want to save your image as your screen saver, click the Screen Saver button. In the dialog box that follows you can select where the screen saver file should be saved. Your screen saver file is now immediately activated.

Special paper sizes for panorama pictures

If panorama photos are printed on letter size or legal size paper, big white empty areas remain because of the special format of panorama photos. For this reason, companies such as Agfa and Epson offer paper in panorama format. Agfa offers the "Photo Paper Glossy Panorama" in the sizes 5 7/8" x 14" and 8 1/4" x 23 3/8". The manufacturer offers an interesting service on the Web site www.agfa.com. You can retrieve the best settings to be defined in your printer driver for many printers of different manufacturers from this Web site.

Epson also offers photo paper at a special size of 8 1/4" x 23 3/8". You can find further information on *http://www.epson.com*. You can also find the specific printer driver for your printer on these Web pages.

What should you do if frontal sunlight hits your camera?

You want to take a picture of a fascinating subject and the sun is shining directly towards you – and you don't have a lens hood. This situation is one of the most difficult ones in photography. Because the light meter takes the overall light intensity into consideration, the actual main subject of your picture turns out too dark. A solution to this problem does exist, however: Use your light meter or the internal automatic function of your camera to measure the light. Then take a series of about four pictures of your subject and manually decrease the f stop, which was suggested by your camera by one stop each time you take a picture. If the light meter suggests an f stop of 16, for instance, take your first shot at f16, the next one at f11, the next one at f8, and so on. Don't worry if the camera indicates an error of exposure. If you are using an automatic camera that does not allow you to set your aperture manually, you might find a plus/minus correction feature on your camera that you can set to plus 1 or plus 2, and so on.

Backlit portraits have a fascinating effect. In this case, measure the light intensity directly in front of the subject, step away again, and take the picture with the previously obtained settings.

Conveniently removing people and objects from pictures

If you want to retouch large grainy areas, scratches, or other irregularities such as unattractive street signs, you need a special retouching tool. One tool offered by all of the popular image-editing programs is the stamp tool. Paint Shop Pro uses the term *Clone Brush* to describe this tool. Although different programs might use different names for the stamp tool, the basic principle stays the same. First, an image area is selected that is defined as the source of the copying procedure. Next, you "stamp" over the section to be retouched. The tool is usually displayed as a stamp symbol or a double brush symbol.

1 Open the picture in Paint Shop Pro that you want to retouch. In this example, you want to remove the person from the picture.

2 First, enable the *Clone Brush* tool. It is the 11th tool from the top in the toolbar.

3 Open the *Tool Options* window to define the size and properties of the tool. From the *Shape* options, select a brush shape according to your needs. The *Round* option is illustrated. With some subjects, it might make more sense to choose another shape such as *Left Slash* or *Horizontal*. You also need to select a size that is appropriate for your subject. A brush size of 30 was used for this project.

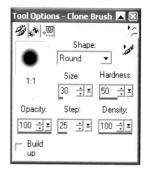

Setting a static source area or letting it wander with your mouse

If you enable the *Aligned* option, the specified source area moves – based on the movement of your mouse; distance and direction stay the same. It is usually more practical to select the *Non-Aligned* option because you have better control over your retouching procedure this way. If you release the mouse and click the image again, the previously defined source area is used for the cloning. You should define the source area more often if you want to retouch other tonal values.

---

4 The *Tool Options* window contains a second tab – the *Clone Brush Options*. Here you can decide whether you want to use the *Aligned* or *Non-Aligned* option. The option *Aligned* is illustrated for this image. You should test the different effects of both functions.

5 Now look for an image section to be retouched. In this case it is the back of the person. Specify the source area that should be copied on top of this section by right-clicking it. This example shows the sky was right-clicked.

6 Next, press and hold the mouse button to copy the previously selected source area on top of the target area. Start at the outer edge of the subject and move towards the middle of the target area.

7 If you are working on difficult areas, it is important to choose a high zoom factor and to work with a small brush tip.

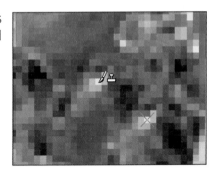

8 Working with the clone brush tool might appear difficult at first. It is a good idea to practice on relatively simple subjects first, and after a short period of time you can do even complicated retouching procedures without difficulty.

Retouching gradients

If the image's flaw is located in a section containing color gradients, that is, smooth transitions, the retouching procedure might be more difficult. You must redefine the source area regularly and approach the gradient carefully. There is always a visible edge, however. If this is the case, reduce the opacity level to 50%, for instance. Use a relatively large brush tip if possible and repaint the edge at low opacity. This way you can create smooth transitions.

The scratch remover tool in Paint Shop Pro

Paint Shop Pro offers a special tool for the correction of small dust or scratches – the *Scratch Remover* tool. Select the tool; click in front of the scratch or dust; click and hold your mouse and drag the cross-hair symbol across the scratch. Paint Shop Pro then fills the selected section with the surrounding color. This tool also works well

with color gradients. It is not suitable for image areas containing distinct structures or patterns as they would be considered scratches or fluff and removed. In some image areas, you might need to apply the tool more often to remove the scratch.

4. Goodbye bunny eyes – and other simple retouching secrets

Multi-purpose photographs: The first printouts and more

If you have taken your pictures, transferred them to your PC, and edited them, you probably want to do more than just display them on the monitor and send them over e-mail. You probably want to print them. In this chapter, you learn how to save space while printing on the right paper and how to create greeting and business cards in Paint Shop Pro.

Printing your edited pictures for the first time

If you want to print your pictures, first decide if you want only a trial printout (for example, for your archive) or if you want a photo-quality printout. The paper selection (paper type, whether glossy or matte) depends on the intended use.

Unlike slides, pictures taken with a digital camera have only a limited resolution. For this reason, they cannot be enlarged at will. This doesn't mean that digital photographs have a lower quality than analog ones. If you stick with a resolution of 200 to 300 dpi and use the right paper, you can achieve outstanding results.

Determining the maximum picture size with Paint Shop Pro

1 Open a picture that you have loaded from your digital camera in Paint Shop Pro. The sample picture is 3 megapixels.

2 Select the command *Image/Resize*. In the *Actual/Print size* area, you can see the current picture measurements at a resolution of 72 dpi.

3 Click in the check box next to *Maintain aspect ratio of* to disable this option. This is important, because you only want to redistribute the existing pixels at a new resolution.

4 Enter the desired resolution in the field of the same name. For a standard inkjet printout, 200 dpi is enough. For high-resolution device, enter 300 dpi.

5 Notice that Paint Shop Pro has redistributed the total number of pixels to a new resolution, which has resulted in a smaller number of inches in the *Actual/print size* area. The new values are the print measurements that you can achieve with the new resolution.

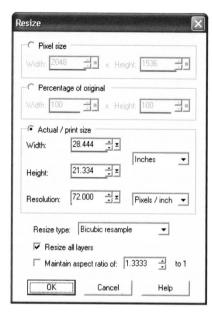
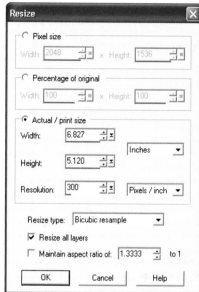

Image resolution versus printing resolution

The printing resolution must be higher than the image resolution because the printer uses more than one of its pixels to create one monitor pixel. For instance, one orange pixel on screen is composed of several yellow on magenta pixels in print.

Selecting the right paper

Selecting the right paper is almost as important for the quality of the printout as selecting the optimum resolution. Your image has the desired sharpness only if the paper can absorb the ink correctly. Regular paper absorbs ink, so the colors bleed. In the meantime, many papers are available on the market; the following is an overview.

Pay attention to the manufacturer's recommendations

If you are unsure, trust the printer manufacturer's recommendations about which papers to use. All elements that influence a printer's performance – ink density, printer head performance, and paper surface – have been matched by the manufacturer.

5. Multi-purpose photographs: The first printouts and more

Regular paper

Use regular copy paper to print out overviews of your pictures. This paper has several disadvantages. The first one is its high absorbency. The ink bleeds and dark areas look like they are stained. The other problem is the wood content of this paper. Regular paper fades in light and yellows even behind glass fast.

Glossy PE-coated paper

The surface of PE-coated paper is sealed to keep the ink from being absorbed. The color droplets remain on the surface. For this reason, the paper takes longer to dry, and the printout is more sensitive to environmental influences. The quality of the printout is good, however.

Cast-coated glossy paper

Glossy paper comes in different weights; its finish ranges from high glossy to matte. With this paper, the ink is absorbed by the surface immediately and dries quickly. Printouts on this type of paper are considerably less photo-sensitive and more resistant to environmental influences.

Constant innovation

Because the resolutions and quality of inkjet printers are ever increasing, the manufacturers need new arguments for selling their products. The newest catchword is now the longevity of the printouts. For this reason, always pay attention to the information on the photo-sensitivity of both paper and ink. The newest innovations already make it possible for inkjet printouts to last up to 20 years. You should protect your pictures from direct exposure to sunlight, however. Keeping them behind glass also increases their longevity.

Tip

Data Becker paper

Data Becker offers you a multitude of specialty papers, ranging from high glossy, lightweight to heavyweight photo paper. Data Becker's range of papers is designed for different uses. In addition to the standard assortment, you can also find papers for special uses, such as CD labels, business cards, or transfers for T-shirt printing. For printing pictures without a margin, you can use perforated papers in different sizes. To order paper online, go to *www.databecker.com*.

Printing tips

When you are buying a printer, think about whether you want a model that has separate cartridges for each color. It often happens that magenta runs out, while cyan and yellow are still half full. If you have a printer with individual cartridges, you must change the magenta cartridge at this point. This way, you can save quite a bit of money. Ask your printer manufacturer for information about the newest models.

If your printer won't print, sometimes all that's needed is patience. For instance, an image file might have been selected and the *File/Print* command clicked repeatedly. It could take the printer about 20 trial prints for the fine print head nozzles to be filled and the colors to look right.

Use high-quality paper that is suitable for your device.

Make sure the printer cartridges are installed correctly.

Pay attention to the manufacturer's warnings. Sometimes, for instance, the ink cartridges cannot be removed until they are empty. Otherwise, when you put them back in, the printer thinks they are empty and asks for new cartridges.

An important thing to remember is that you shouldn't overburden your printer with paper that is too thick for it. Thick papers can seriously damage the sensitive paper feed mechanism. Definitely observe the manufacturer's recommendations for paper thickness.

If you are not sure whether to check off portrait or landscape in the *Print* dialog box, try out which one works best by printing out a sample on cheap paper.

For the best printouts, make sure that you have chosen the highest possible resolution for your printer in the *Print* dialog box. This might lengthen the printing process.

If the printing quality happens to be bad or if you have a color cast, one of your colors might have run out or one of your cartridges might be blocked.

If you haven't used your printer for a long time, remember that ink remains can block parts of the print head. Depending on your printer model, there are different ways of servicing it. Use the manual that came with your printer or contact the manufacturer's technical support desk.

Business cards with your own picture

Add your picture to your business card, and the recipient is certain to remember you. In this chapter, you learn how to do this.

The right clothes for your portrait

Clothing choice is one of the most important aspects of portrait photography. Your face should be the lightest area in the picture, so don't wear white. It draws attention away from your face. When you are looking at portraits, try to discover the effects of differently colored clothing.

1 Start Paint Shop Pro and go to *File/New*. In the following dialog box, enter 3.5 × 2.0 inches as the card dimensions and select a resolution of 300 dpi. Select *White* as the *Background color* and *16.7 Million Colors* as the *Image type*.

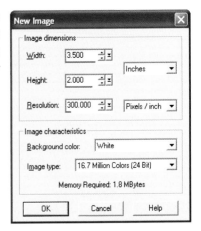

Determining the size of your business cards

The size of your business cards is more important than it seems at first. The most convenient size for business cards is approximately that of credit cards, or about 3.5 × 2.0 inches. This way, you can be sure that your business card fits in any business card holder and is not thrown out because it is too large. On the other hand, an unusual shape or size can grab attention. Make your choice depending on how you use your card. Whether you print your cards in landscape or portrait orientation is entirely up to you.

2 You now have an empty file showing a white background. In it, insert a textured background. Go to *Effects/Texture Effects/Texture*. Select a texture from the list. The example shows the first standard texture.

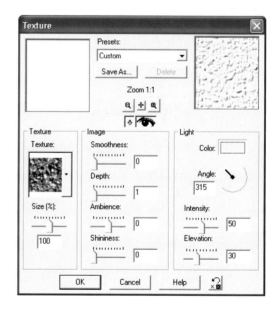

The resolution for business cards

As previously mentioned, 200 dpi is usually enough for printing a picture with an inkjet printer. However, when you are working with text, increase the resolution to 300 or even 400 dpi just to be certain. Text is as sensitive to a low resolution as line drawings. The aliasing is especially visible here.

3 Open your passport picture. We now want to copy it into the business card by going to *Selections/Select All*. Once the picture is selected, copy it to the clipboard by going to *Edit/Copy*.

4 Click the business card file. Insert the picture from the clipboard by going to *Edit/Paste/As New Layer*. To activate the *Layer* palette, right-click a palette or toolbar and then select the *Layer Palette* option from the pop-up menu.

5 Edit your passport picture any way you like on its own layer. For instance, you can move it around with the *Mover* tool (the fifth tool from the top in the toolbar).

6 Because the size of the picture is probably not ideal, enable the *Deformation* tool (the third tool from the top in the toolbar). Your picture is now framed by a selection rectangle. Right-click one of the corners and drag it with your mouse. You are now rescaling the layer without distorting the picture. (It is important to rescale with the right mouse button and not with the left, because with the left button the picture might become distorted.)

7 Place your portrait on the business card. Make sure that the eyes are drawn to the center of the card.

Note

Scaling with the Deformation tool

Scaling image data inside a layer also leads to a new computation of the pixels and therefore to a certain loss in detail and sharpness. However, this is almost not recognizable when you only alter the picture once, but you shouldn't repeat this process too often.

8 Enable the *Text* tool in the toolbar (it is represented by the letter A), and click inside the image. The text editor opens. Enter the desired text in the editor, for example, name, address, phone number, and e-mail address.

9 Format the text by selecting the desired letters or words with the mouse, then applying different attributes – such as font, font size and style. In the example, the name was entered first and then the editor was closed, and finally it was clicked with the *Text* tool again. This way, two separate text frames were created that can be moved independently from each other.

10 Design the business card according to your own vision. The example shows a line with the *Draw* tool and created the ellipse with the *Preset Shapes* tool. The *Draw* tool uses a foreground color. You can choose the attributes for both tools from the *Tool* palette.

Moving text in Paint Shop Pro

If you want to move a text frame in Paint Shop Pro, hover with the *Text* tool above the text frame until you see an A in brackets. Now you can click and drag the text frame to a new position.

Printing your business card

You have now created a business card. If you print this single card, you are wasting a lot of paper. However, you have different possibilities for printing several business cards on one sheet of paper. You can create a page in the size of the paper and copy the card on this page several times. In Paint Shop Pro, the simplest method is to use the *Print Multiple Images* feature.

1 At this point, the different objects that make up your business card are located on different layers. Save this version as a Paint Shop Pro image. In the PSP format, all layers are kept intact and you can change them individually at a later time.

2 Now select the command *Layers/Merge/Merge All (Flatten)*. With this command, all layers are merged into one. Go to *File/Save* and save the card as a TIF file.

3 Now you can print. Go to *File/Print Multiple Images*. A dialog window opens with a preview of your business card on the left and the printable area on the right. Drag the card to the printable area as many times as you want. First, however, activate a grid that helps you position your cards.

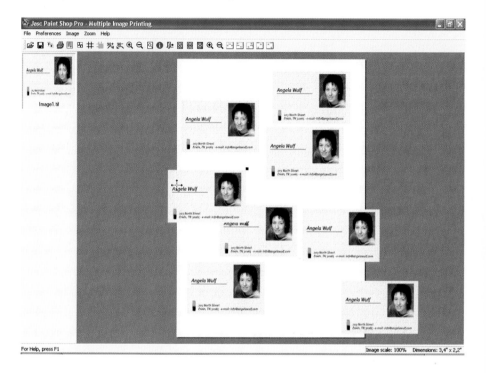

4 Go to *Preferences/Options*. Unfortunately, you can't define the spacing between pictures or cut marks automatically in Paint Shop Pro. For this reason, you must use a trick: Define the individual cell a little larger than the cards. Then, align each card at the top left corner of its cell.

5 Enable the *Show grid* and *Snap to grid* options. Enter the following values in the *Grid Settings* area: *Horizontal Spacing 3.6* inches and *Vertical spacing 2.5* inches. The grid cells are thus larger than the cards, so you can position the cards better.

5. Multi-purpose photographs: The first printouts and more

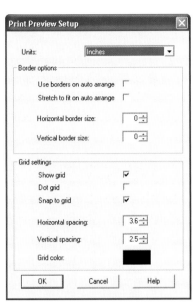

6 Drag a card into each cell (aligned with the top left corner). Select the *File/Print* command to print the page on your default printer. At this point, you also have the possibility, however, of defining further print options. Paint Shop Pro gives you the standard settings for your printer.

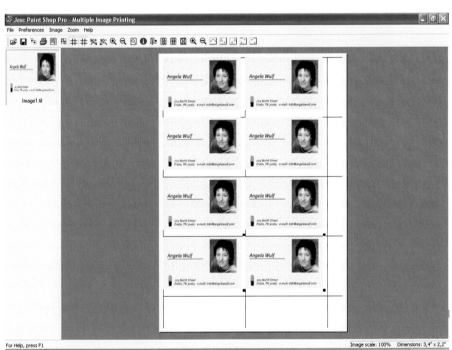

30,000 Business Cards from Data Becker

Data Becker has developed a complete solution for printing business cards. You can select from 30,000 layouts, from serious business cards to appealing personal cards. Using the program from layout to printed result is intuitive, and you can order either just the program CD or the bundle version with special paper online at *www. databecker.com*.

Saving space when printing

In the above example, you printed multiple copies of one business card. Yet the *Print Multiple Images* function in Paint Shop Pro is just as helpful if you want to print pictures of different formats.

1 Go to *File/Open* and open several pictures – as many as you want to put on one page.

2 Select the command *File/Print multiple Images*. On the left, notice a list of your pictures. Click each picture and drag it to the page preview on the right. You can even drag a picture several times onto the page.

3 If the auxiliary lines bother you during this free positioning, go to *Preferences/Options* and deselect the *Show grid* option.

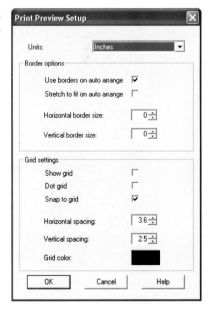

5. Multi-purpose photographs: The first printouts and more

4 Drag as many pictures onto the page as you want to print in this size. Arrange the pictures as desired. If you click and drag the corners of your pictures, you can resize them as you want. However, you shouldn't enlarge any picture by more than 20%; otherwise, the sharpness is diminished.

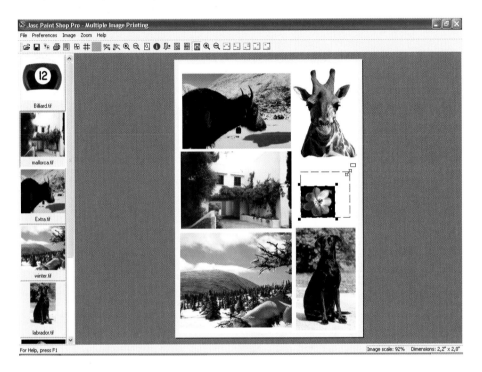

5 When everything is in its place, select *File/Print*. The page is printed on your default printer with the current settings. No other print dialog box opens.

Greeting cards in Paint Shop Pro

Surprise your correspondents with homemade greeting cards. With the pictures you took with your digital camera and Paint Shop Pro as your platform, you can design your own cards in no time. And the best part: You can send out the same card to several people just by changing the name.

You must decide beforehand which format you want to print your cards in, that is, whether you want them to be simple or folding cards. Here, you create one 4 × 5 folding card and then print two copies of it on the same piece of paper (just change the name for the second card). This means that you are creating a cover and an inside. Then print each on both sides of the paper.

5. Multi-purpose photographs: The first printouts and more

1 Open a picture you like. The image in our example is 3 × 3 inches. Add a special frame and text to it.

2 First, apply an atmospheric illumination effect to the picture by going to *Effects/Illumination Effects/Sunburst*.

3 Then, insert the frame *Photo Edge 01* by going to *Image/Picture Frame*. This frame is practical because it is inserted on its own layer and can be edited independently from the background image.

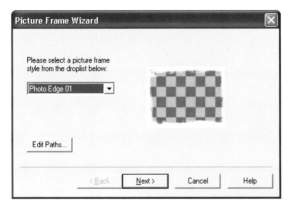

4 Next, apply a grid to the frame by selecting the command *Effects/Texture Effects/Mosaic-Antique*. (You must move the preview images with the mouse to see the edges of the picture.)

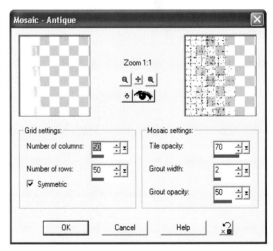

5 Enable the *Text* tool and click into the picture to open the text editor. Type in your text. To separate the individual lines, press Enter.

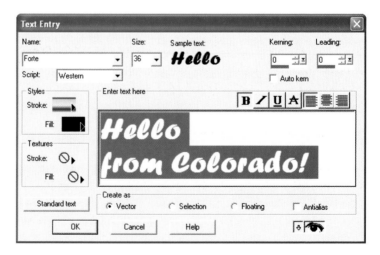

6 Because you want to apply a filter to the text layer as well, convert it to a raster layer with the *Layers/Convert to Raster Layer* command. Paint Shop Pro then converts the vector layer to a pixel layer. Apply the *Effects/Texture Effects/Emboss* command to your text.

7 If you are happy with the way you have edited the individual layers, merge them with the command *Layers/Merge/Merge All (Flatten)* to a single background layer.

8 Create a new file for the inside of the greeting card. Remember that text is a lot more sensitive to low resolution than images. For this reason, use a resolution of 300 dpi for the inside (which is only text).

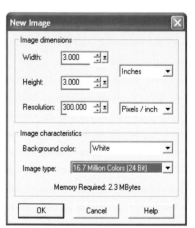

9 For the cover and inside to line up in the completed card, turn the inside text upside down. To do so, go to *Image/Rotate*. Under *Degrees*, check *180* and then click *OK*.

10 Select *File/Print Multiple Images*, to arrange the two images in the print area. In this case, arrange the images to print out two cards at once. The cover and back of each card is on one side of the paper, the inside of the card on the other side. Print the first side out; then turn the paper to print out the other side. (The cover and back of one card is on the same side of the paper as the inside of the other card.) Then, you only have to cut the cards along the bottom/top to separate them from each other.

11 Go to *Preferences/Options* to open a dialog box in which you can define auxiliary lines to help you place the images.

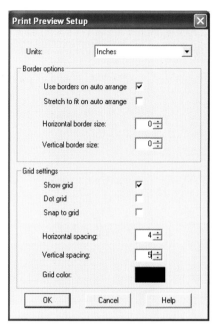

12 The two open files appear once again on the left of the screen. Drag the images to the print area and position them.

13 Select the *File/Print* command to initiate the printing process. After one side is printed, turn the printout along its vertical axis; then feed it back into the printer to print on the back side of the paper. (You should also remember to change the name for the second print.)

14 To separate the cards, use a ruler and an exacto knife. Because you have to make only one cut here, separating the cards is easy. When you create more complicated layouts, insert light gray cut marks.

5. Multi-purpose photographs: The first printouts and more

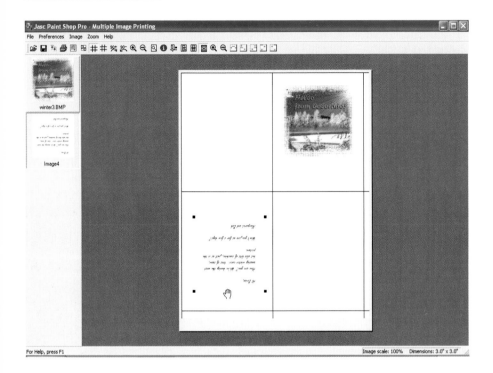

Filters and close-up lenses

Some camera objectives have step-rings for attaching filters or lenses. For all other cameras, you can buy mounts that you can put in front of the objective. The only problem: you must remove the mount before turning off the camera; otherwise, you might have problems retracting the objective.

Close-ups

If your camera doesn't have a macro mode, shooting close-ups can be quite a challenge. Often, the subject becomes blurry the moment you come within a yard of it. In this case, the solution is a close-up lens. Close-up lenses are available in most photo stores. If you want to look for lenses on the Internet, you can find lenses for many camera models in the *Photographic Equipment* category at *http://kohscamera.com*. If your camera isn't listed here, go to the manufacturer's Web site. At *http://photogra phy-on-the.net/forum/search.php?action=viewtoday*, you can find a forum where you can formulate your own questions about lenses. The site is frequently visited, which means that your questions are answered fast.

5. Multi-purpose photographs: The first printouts and more

Viewing your photos on your TV

Intuitively, you might link digital photography with presenting images on your computer. But how would you present your photos if no PC is available? All cameras with a video out can transfer photos to your TV. This way you can transfer your digital photos into the living room of your friends without any problems.

Objects behind glass

If you want to take a picture of an object that is located behind glass, the glass is an obstacle to your camera's flash. Often, the picture only shows the reflection of the flash hitting the glass. You have two options to solve this problem. Use a lens hood; go up to the glass and take the picture at a distance of approximately 3 to 4 cm away from the glass. The second option is to stand sideways to the glass and take the picture from there. This way the reflection is diverted.

Fill flash

If it's a bright and sunny day and you want to take a picture of a subject in the shade or one that is backlit, the use of a fill flash is recommended. You have to be careful with built-in flashes, however, as they usually don't have the required strength. If you are more than a couple of yards away, a built-in flash is usually useless.

Your photo presentation on TV

To connect your digital camera to your TV set, you must take the following points into consideration: The camera must have a video output that has to be connected to the video input of your TV by a cable. It is particularly useful if your camera offers you the option of transferring images that were edited on your PC – for instance, by applying filters or adding text – back to the camera to present these images on your TV.

6. Viewing your photos on your TV

TV screens have a lower resolution

TV screens have a considerably lower resolution than computer screens. If you want to view your pictures on your TV screen only, it is sufficient to take them at a relatively low resolution. This way it takes less time for the pictures to be displayed entirely on the TV screen.

1 Connect the TV and your camera with a video cable. The cable provided with your camera contains an RCA plug that must be connected to the video input of your TV. You can acquire this adapter in TV or electronics stores.

The TV as your selection tool

Especially when you are on vacation, it is not always possible to transfer your pictures to a PC, and the storage capacity of your storage media limits the amount of pictures you can take. It is therefore useful to view the images on a large TV screen to pre-select your images, because evaluating the pictures on a small camera display screen is not always easy. This way you save space for really good pictures.

Power supply through a wall adapter

If you are using your camera in a stationary manner – for instance, to present your images on TV – you should power your camera through a wall adapter. You save the power of your batteries this way.

2 The pictures are now displayed on the TV screen instead of your camera's display screen. Usually, you can turn off the display of image data – in case it bothers you. Your camera's manual tells you how to do that. The pictures can be played back the same way as you would view them one after the other on your camera's display screen. Some cameras, however, also offer a slide show function. This auto-play mode allows you to program the playback of the images.

3 If you are using a digital camera capable of recording audio material, you can transfer the audio data through an AV cable. An AV cable is capable of transferring image as well as audio data.

Note

Pictures in portrait format are tilted

If you are taking pictures specifically for presentations on screen, you should take into consideration that pictures in portrait format automatically appear tilted on your TV screen.

Note

Interesting links about digital photography

Because the field of digital photography is rapidly advancing, visit good Web sites once in a while to find out about new developments. On *http://www.steves-digicams.com* you can find new developments and tests from the world of digital photography. You should also check out *http://www.dpreview.com* – Phil Askey is also looking at the current developments of digital cameras and their peripheral equipment. The test reports are particularly extensive; they won't spare you any details.

Creating photo CDs with Movie Maker

Windows Movie Maker is provided with Windows ME and XP. It is a convenient tool to download pictures from your digital camera and to create a slide show. You can even add background sound to your slide show if you have a microphone (or by using existing, saved files). Once the slide show is finished, burn it on CD and present it on other PCs.

1 Start Windows Movie Maker by selecting *Start/All Programs/Accessories/Windows Movie Maker.*

2 Select *File/Import.* In the dialog box that follows, you can either select the drive of your digital camera or an image folder on your hard disk. By the way, you can also import images from different folders. Select *File/Import* again and navigate to another folder. After the import procedure, the images are added.

3 Select *Edit/Select All.* Your images are now selected and the first image is displayed on Movie Maker's monitor. If you click *Start* below the movie window, the slide show plays back.

6. Viewing your photos on your TV

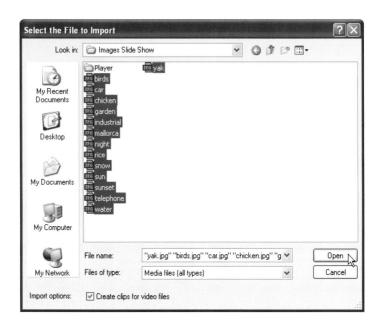

Managing images with Movie Maker

The managing of images in Movie Makers works similar to ACDSee. Select *View/Collections* to display the navigation window for the collections in the left area. Here, you can create new collections and move images by dragging and dropping them.

E-mailing a movie

If you don't even want to save the movie but instead want to e-mail it to a friend, select *File/Send Movie To/E-mail*. The movie is then generated, your standard e-mail program is started, and you can send the e-mail as usual.

4 Select *View/Storyboard* now. All of the selected images are now listed in the storyboard. Left-click these thumbnails and move them by pressing and holding the mouse button. This way you can change the sequence of your slide show in a snap.

5 By default, each image displays for five seconds. If you want to change the display time, go to *View/Options*. You can define the display time of an image by changing the *photo duration* time in the dialog box that follows.

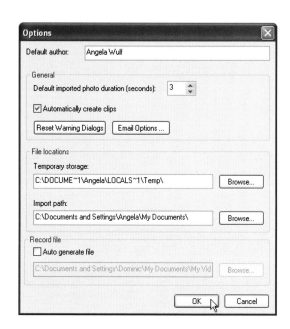

Merging video clips from your digital camera

If your camera is capable of recording video sequences, you can cross-fade individual clips in Windows Movie Maker. In timeline view, click the second clip of the two video clips to be cross-faded. Now drag the second clip on top of the first one. The gray area indicates the cross-fade time. The time duration of a transition cannot exceed the duration of an adjacent clip.

6 If you want to save your movie now to burn it onto CD, select *File/Save Movie*. In the dialog box that follows, you can select the quality of the movie; add a title, the author's name, as well as any commentaries. Then click *OK*. The usual Windows Save As dialog box appears in which you can save the movie in WMV format on your hard disk.

When the sun sinks into the ocean

It is a fascinating task to capture the colors of a sunset. When looking at the light meter, you notice an underexposure of 2 stops. Don't correct this setting, however, as the colors of the sunset appear richer when underexposed.

7 If you burn the movie on CD, you can transfer it to other PCs without any problems and play it back with Windows Media Player. If you are working with a DVD system, you can also save the file on DVD and play it back on a DVD player.

Inserting images into text files

Most digital cameras create images at a resolution of 72 or 96 dpi. The overall number of pixels is distributed over many inches and file sizes of 28 x 21 inches, for instance, are obtained if a 3 mega pixel camera is used. If you insert such an image in MS Word, for instance, by using the commands *Insert/Picture/From File*, the image is too big and almost explodes off the page. In such a case, you can use the command *Image/ Resize* in Paint Shop Pro, for example, to recalculate the width the image should have in the text file. Please make sure, however, that you only change the *Resolution* value, for example, increase the value to *300 Pixel/Inch*. This way, the pixels are redistributed automatically and a new image width is created. The overall amount of pixels – discernible from the *Pixel size* section – should not be changed because doing so would cause a definite loss in quality.

6. Viewing your photos on your TV

Slide shows and Web publishing

In this chapter you learn how to present your images on a monitor. You are introduced to a program called PhotoFlicks, which is published by Data Becker. This program allows you to burn your slide shows on CDs. The second section of this chapter teaches you how to create a simple HTML site to publish your pictures on the Net. In addition, you learn how to save your images with transparent background, how to create background tiles for your Web site, and how to e-mail your pictures.

PhotoFlicks

Why not create an exciting multimedia show with your digital pictures? PhotoFlicks allows you to conveniently admire your favorite pictures on TV. Load your images directly from your camera, beef them up with astounding image and sound effects, and burn your show on a video CD that can be played back with a DVD player.

7. Slide shows and Web publishing

Archiving images on CD

With PhotoFlicks you cannot only create slide shows – you can also burn unedited images on CD. In this case, an image viewer is also burned onto the CD. You can obtain the program from *www.databecker.com*, for instance.

1 Install Data Becker's PhotoFlicks on your Computer. Double-click the Setup.exe file on the CD. An installation wizard guides you through the required steps.

2 Start Data Becker's PhotoFlicks now. A wizard greets you again and asks you to assign a name to your first PhotoFlick project.

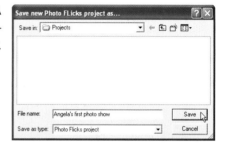

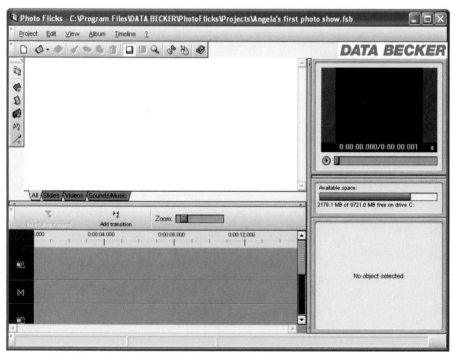

3 On the top left, you can see the album window that displays all of the files you want to use for your PhotoFlicks project: images, music or vocal recordings, or movies. The timeline window, which is used to arrange your material to create a movie, is located on the bottom left. The movie preview window allows you to preview your slide shows; it is located on the top right. The section underneath displays the available disk space. The section on the bottom right displays the cross-fade effects applied to the arranged tracks. Because you just started the program, this section remains blank.

4 Go to *Album/Add file to album* to add files to your album. You can now choose and open as many files as desired. The files are then displayed as slides in the album window.

5 Go to *Edit/Select All* to select all slides; select *Timeline/Insert object from album into timeline* to add the images to your slide show. The images are now displayed in the timeline window. Use the *Zoom* slider above the timeline to define the size of the images displayed in the timeline window.

The buttons in PhotoFlicks

The buttons from top to bottom have the following functions:

 Create blank slide

 Add all folders to album

 Add file to album

 Retrieve pictures from scanner/camera and add

 Create a new slide from a text and add

 Record sound and add

Note

125

7. Slide shows and Web publishing

6 Click *Start* located underneath the preview window on the top right to start the preview of your slide show. The images are not displayed one after the other, because the program creates automatic cross-fades between each image. Click the button again to stop the preview.

7 You can now define the display time of each single image as well as the transition between the images. To change the display time of a slide, click it in the timeline. You can define the display time at the bottom right.

8 If you want to change a transition, click the corresponding transition symbol between two images on the timeline. Then select the desired type of transition from the window on the bottom right. Click *Preview* to preview the transition.

9 Save your slide show by selecting *Project/Save*; then burn your project to CD by selecting *Project/Create CD*. A wizard guides you through the required steps again.

Adding images to an HTML site – and what you must keep in mind

Apart from choosing the lowest possible file size, the correct referencing of your image file is of the utmost importance when inserting images in an HTML file. Referencing sounds is complicated; however, it means that your HTML site has to know the location the image should be loaded from. The image file can be in the same directory as the HTML file or it can be located in a subdirectory. Prepare the images first to present them over the Internet, whereby you must find the golden mean between quality and file size. Afterwards, create a simple HTML site containing a two-column table in which you can insert your images.

Preparing images in Paint Shop Pro

On the Internet it is particularly important that images are displayed as quickly as possible. Consequently, the images have to be saved in a compressed format such as JPG or PNG. Although the image quality suffers from the compression, you cannot avoid this compromise.

1 Create a directory on your hard disk, for example, *C:\ImagesInternet* in which you save the HTML page and all corresponding images.

2 Start Paint Shop Pro and open the images you want to place on your Web site.

3 Select *File/Save As* and look for the desired directory – in this case *C:\ ImagesInternet*. Select the *JPEG – JFIF Compliant* file format from the bottom list box. Then click *Options* in the lower right of the dialog box.

4 The *Save Options* dialog box allows you to control the compression factor; however, no preview of the compressed image is displayed. Therefore, click *Run optimizer*.

5 Under *Set compression value to*, you can select the appropriate compression value by trying out different values. Use the preview window to find the highest possible compression rate at the best possible image quality. Once you have found a satisfactory value, click the *Download Times* tab to find out about the file size of the optimized file and its download time at different modem settings.

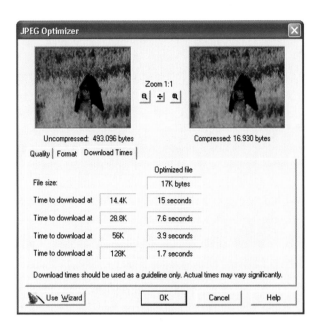

6 If you are satisfied with the settings, confirm them with OK. Proceed the same way to save all of the desired images in the corresponding directory.

Inserting images in an HTML table

Once you have optimized your images, insert them in your HTML page.

Finding HTML editors

You can find a large selection of HTML editors – shareware as well as freeware – on the Web site www.bluechillies.com.

Creating the basic HTML structure

You can create the basic HTML structure by using an HTML editor such as Dreamweaver or Web Weaver or by copying the following text into a Windows Notepad document and saving the file with the file extension .htm or .html.

Adding images to an HTML site – and what you must keep in mind

1 Start your HTML editor or Windows Notepad. First, create the following basic structure for your empty HTML site:

2 It is easier to place your images by inserting them into a table. This way you can add your commentaries next to each image. You could insert a table with two columns and three rows, for instance: The <tr> and </tr> tags indicate the table row and the <td> and </td> tags indicate the individual cells of a row. The table tags have to be placed between the <body> and </body> tags.

3 Between the <td> and </td> tags, you must insert the image source tag or you can insert text. The image source tag reads: <img src="mon_01.jpg">. mon_01.jpg is the file name of the sample image used here. You must enter the file name of your image instead. The text and images inserted alternate vertically.

4 After you copy the HTML code, insert the file names of your images and save the code as an html file in the same directory as your images. Your Web site looks as follows:

Paying attention to correct file referencing

In the example, the command <img src="filename.jpg"> is inserted in the image in the HTML file. The images must be located in the same directory as the HTML file. If you want to save the images in a separate subdirectory of your HTML file directory (for example, PICS), the image source code has to refer to the corresponding directory as follows: <img src="PICS/filename.jpg">. The PICS directory has to be placed in front of the file name; a / symbol has to separate the directory and the file name.

In the left example, all files are located in one directory. If you use this folder struc-ture, the images' source code reads <img src="filename.jpg". In the example on the right, the subdirectory *PICS was created. Consequently, the image source code* <img src="PICS/filename.jpg"> has to be used.

Creating a transparent background for your images

If you want to display an object that was extracted from an image, that is, an image with a transparent background, on your Web page, you must save this image in GIF or PNG format. These formats support transparency – unlike the JPG or BMP format.

1 Open an image in Paint Shop Pro in which the background should be removed and which should be displayed on a Web page with a transparent background. When doing this project, it is important that you work with a copy of the original image. You still have a back-up copy this way in case you accidentally erase some-thing.

2 If your image is on a background layer, it is important to promote the back-ground layer to a regular layer as background layers do not support transparency. Select the commands *Layers/Promote to Layer* for this purpose.

3 Select the *Eraser* tool. Open the Tool Options window and select a suit-able shape and size for your eraser.

4 Start erasing the background from your image. You should change the tool tip in case you want to erase larger or stray areas, for instance. Paint Shop Pro indicates the transparent areas with a checkered pattern.

5 Once you have extracted the entire object, select the command File/Save As. Select the entry *CompuServe Graphics Interchange* (*.gif) from the list box at the far bottom. Then, click *Options* and *Run Optimizer*.

6 Make sure the *Transparency* tab is selected and enable the option *Existing image or layer transparency*. Confirm the dialog box with *OK*.

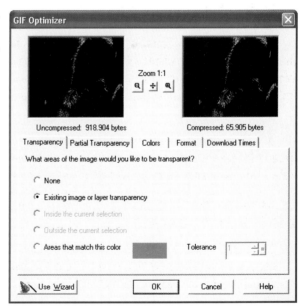

7 If you place your image on a Web site, the background of the image is now transparent.

Tiling images like a pro to create a beautiful background

When working with the Internet, small file sizes and consequently fast loading times are of utmost importance. If you want to create attractive backgrounds, you don't need to create images at a size of 800 × 600 pixels, for instance. You can create smaller images and use your HTML editor or the browser to automatically tile the entire background area with the small image. It is important that the transitions between the individual background tiles are smooth to prevent visible image edges. Numerous Web sites offer background tiles for download. Enter the words background tile + download in a search engine such as www.google.com, for instance, and you can obtain many results. If you want to create your own backgrounds, proceed as follows:

Tile size can be chosen freely

There is no particular reason a tile size of 1 × 5 pixels was chosen for this example. Depending on how intensive you want your pattern to be, adjust the size accordingly. When creating backgrounds, it is important that the contrasts of the background pattern are not too strong; otherwise, it is difficult to read the Web site's text.

1 It is advantageous to use small background tiles as the loading time is reduced enormously. In this example, you create the most spartan type of tiles. Select *File/New*. Enter the values *1* and *5* in the *Width* and *Height* fields, respectively. Select a resolution of *72 Pixels/inch* and confirm your selections with *OK*.

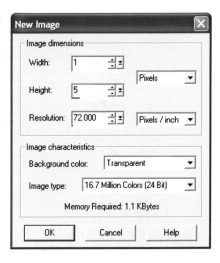

2 Click the *Paint Brush* tool and select a brush tip size of *1 Pixel* in the *Tool Options* window.

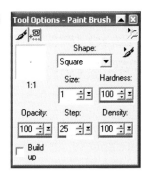

3 Click the *Color Palette* to select a color. Then color one pixel of the tile file with the chosen color.

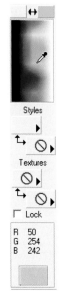

4 Change the color afterwards. The brightness level of this color should not deviate too much from the previously chosen one. Apply this color to further pixels. It is always a surprise to find out later on how the pattern appears in the browser after the image has been tiled.

5 Background tiles with a few colors are suited perfectly to be saved as GIF files. Saving in GIF produces small files. Select the commands *File/Save as*. From the bottom list box, select the entry *CompuServe Graphics Interchange (*.gif)*. Then click *Options* and *Run Optimizer*.

6 In the *Colors* tab, enter the number of colors that you used. Switch to the *Download Times* tab. Note that this is a tiny file of only 813 bytes, which does not have a negative effect on the loading speed of your Web site. Confirm the dialog box; the file is now saved.

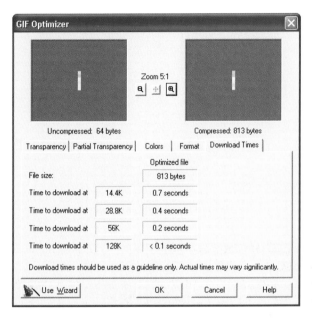

7 You must now insert the tiles in your Web site. It is important that the HTML site and your GIF image are saved in the same directory. You must add the background tag to your HTML code. This tag looks as follows: <body background="back.gif">

The example illustrated here is simple; however, even if you want to create more complicated background patterns, the steps remain the same. Let your imagination soar!

This background tile was created with two colors. The Add Noise effect was added later on.

For this tile, we also inserted irregular lines and dots that were softened by applying the motion blur effect. The result is an interesting looking background tile.

E-mailing images

When e-mailing images, you can choose whether you want to send the image as a file attachment or whether you want to insert it directly into the e-mail body. In the first case, the recipient has to download the image, for instance a JPG file, to his hard disk first to view and possibly edit it in an image viewer such as ACDSee or an image editing program such as Paint Shop Pro. If you insert the image directly in the e-mail body, the recipient sees the image immediately when opening the e-mail.

Sending your file as an attachment

1 Start Outlook Express. Click *Create Mail*. A blank e-mail window opens.

2 Enter the e-mail address of the recipient as well as the subject of the e-mail.

3 Select *Insert/File Attachment*. In the dialog box that follows, look for the saved file.

4 Click *Attach* once you have selected the file. Click *Send* now. The e-mail is now sent, and the recipient can download, view, and edit the file.

Inserting the image directly into the e-mail body

1 If you want the recipient to immediately see the image after opening the e-mail, click *Create Mail* again.

2 This time, select the command *Insert/Picture*. A dialog box opens again.

3 After you select your image and click OK, the image appears directly in the e-mail's body. You can also add any desired text.

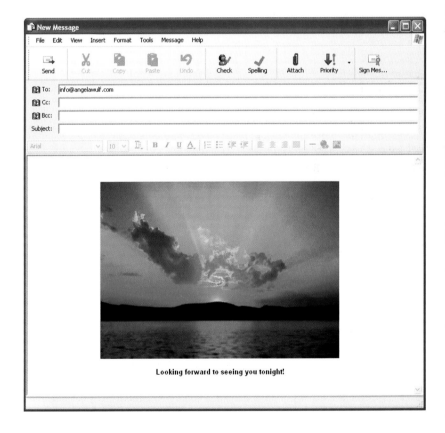

7. Slide shows and Web publishing

Controlling the print quality: Calibrating the monitor and printer

One of the most important tasks when working with digital images is to calibrate the computer system in such a way that the printed colors look just like the colors on the monitor. This may sound obvious, but it is a real task.

The difficulty lies in the fact that monitors use radiant colors (RGB), whereas printers have to convert these colors to pigments (CMYK). On the whole, the CMYK system contains fewer colors than RGB, so some colors (especially light blues and grays) appear different on the printed page. (This subject has also been treated in chapter 2.4). The second reason is that every device, whether it is a digital camera, a scanner, a monitor, or a printer, has its own color cast. These color casts must be adjusted to match each other.

The solution to this problem is called Image Color Management or ICM for short. ICM is a system that uses so-called color profiles to match the color casts of different devices to each other and is an integrated part of Windows since Windows 98. Color profiles are standardized by the International Color Consortium (ICC), for which reason they are also called ICC profiles. Today, ICC profiles are available for almost all input and output devices. In this chapter, you calibrate your monitor in Paint Shop Pro. In the next section, you install ICC profiles. In the last section, you match the profiles in Paint Shop Pro to ensure consistent colors from the display to the printed page when you are using the program.

Monitor calibration in Paint Shop Pro

First define the gamma or contrast of the monitor. In Paint Shop Pro, this is easily done.

1 Go to *File/Preferences/Monitor Gamma*. The image that appears in the dialog box is probably similar to our illustration: the color boxes are clearly discernable from the surrounding dithering pattern.

8. Controlling the print quality: Calibrating the monitor and printer

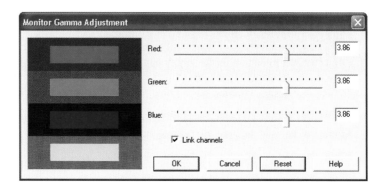

2 The gamma value of the monitor is only ideal, however, when the boxes inside the color fields are indistinguishable from the surrounding areas. Check the box next to *Link channels* and then move the *Red*, *Green*, and *Blue* sliders. You can usually get good results by moving the sliders the same amount. If this should not be the case for you, disable the check box again and adjust the three channels individually.

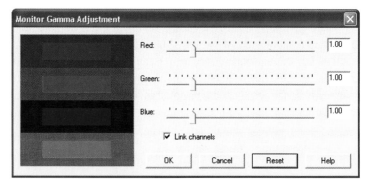

3 When you are happy with the settings, confirm the dialog box. This communicates the particular monitor contrast to the program, and the pictures are displayed on the screen accordingly.

Ensure constant light conditions

In practice it is not easy to keep the light conditions constant. Sunlight entering a room constantly changes the lighting of that room. If you are making intensive color corrections, however, you should do so under light conditions that are as constant as possible. The second important thing to know is that the human eye adapts to color casts (you could say it does an automatic white balance). After a while, you are unable to see color casts anymore. To prevent this situation, take breaks when editing images.

Installing ICC profiles

You must install an ICC profile for each of your devices. Your computer comes with a number of color profiles for compatible monitors; a color profile for your printer or scanner is downloaded onto the hard drive when you install the printer or scanner driver. Unfortunately, not all digital cameras have an ICC profile. If that is true for your camera, install profiles only for your monitor and printer.

1 Start Windows Explorer and navigate to the directory *C:\WINDOWS\ System32\Spool\drivers\color*. This is the directory in which the color profiles are stored. Both the monitor and the printer profiles are located here. Right-click the monitor profile that matches your monitor. This opens a pop-up menu, from which you need to select the first entry, *Install Profile*. This action installs the profile.

Which profile should you install?

Usually, only one printer profile is available for each color printer – the one supplied by the printer driver upon installation. This is an all-purpose profile, but you can also find printer profiles taking into account the particular paper and ink you are using as well as the make and model of the printer on the Internet. For a good selection of generic profiles, visit Jetsoft's www.profilehelp.com. If you download a profile from the Internet, make sure you save it in the same folder. In the case of monitor profiles, you might find the many options in the profiles folder bewildering. Choose the profile that most closely matches the monitor you are using.

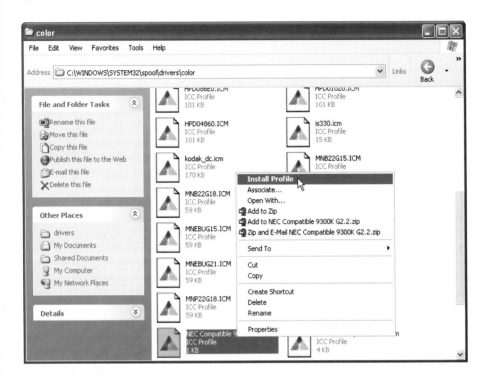

Searching for ICC profiles on the hard drive

If you are working with a system other than Windows XP and are unsure in which directory you need to save your color profiles, search for the term *.ICM in Windows Find. Windows then finds the directory in which the color profiles are located.

2 Next, associate the installed profile with a device. In this case, you want to associate the profile with the monitor. Go to *Start/Control Panel/Appearance and Themes/Display/Settings*. Click *Advanced*. In the dialog box, go to the *Color Management* tab.

3 Click *Add*. Navigate to the profiles folder and select the profile you installed. Confirm your choice.

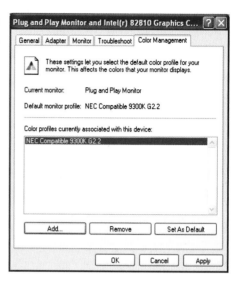

Associating a color profile with the printer

1 To associate a profile with your printer, you first have to install the profile as described above. Then go to *Start/Control Panel/Printers and Other Hardware/Printers and Faxes*. Right-click the printer to which you want to assign a color profile and select the *Properties* entry from the pop-up menu. In the dialog box, click the *Color Management* tab.

2 Check the box next to *Manual* and then click *Add* and select the profile you installed. Your computer system now knows the specific settings for the printer and monitor and adjusts them to each other.

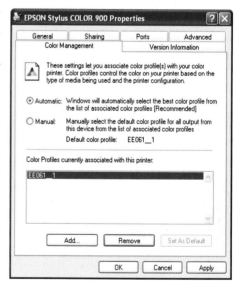

Color management in Paint Shop Pro

As a last step, you must let Paint Shop Pro know the color profiles for your monitor and printer.

1 Go to Paint Shop Pro and select the command *File/Preferences/Color Management*. Check the box next to *Enable Color Management* and then enable the option *Basic Color Management*.

2 From the *Monitor Profile* list box, select the profile you have installed for your monitor. Do the same for the *Printer Profile and* then set the *Rendering Intent* to *Pictures* and confirm the dialog box. Paint Shop Pro has now matched the color profiles for the two devices.

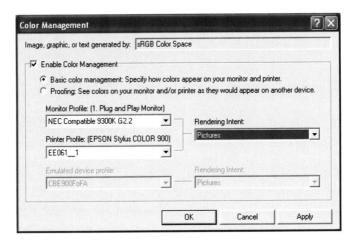

Special Thanks

Special thanks go to Andreas Kaufhold and Christoph Turchetto for their support and collaboration on this book.

8. Controlling the print quality: Calibrating the monitor and printer

Index

Index

Index

Notes

Notes

PhotoFlicks™

TURN YOUR PHOTOS INTO A BRILLIANT MULTIMEDIA SHOW TO WATCH ON YOUR TV!

Software for Windows®

IMPORT
- Easily import any popular image files, or use photos right from your digital camera, scanner or webcam
- Use video clips to add more action to your presentation

EDIT PHOTOS
- Crop, resize, overlap and add special effects to your photos

ARRANGE
- 130 different transitions including fade in and out
- 100 sound effects (WAV and MP3 and music clips)
- 4 audio tracks
- 1000 high quality photos
- Add text with special effects
- Voice-recording: Add your own narration!

OVERVIEW & TIMELINE
- Easily arrange your photos and effects
- Drag and drop your files right into your timeline
- Easily shift whole tracks or individual parts
- Achieve perfect timing by simply stretching the time lengths
- Every image can be rotated, flipped, and more

BURN & PLAY
- Create a video (mpeg) of your creation with a mouse-click and write it as a video CD that can be played on any DVD player
- Easily archive all of your photos & projects onto a CD

Why show family and friends your photos in a dusty album when you can bring them alive with state-of-the-art effects, sound, voice commentary and more – all on your TV? *PhotoFlicks* lets you take your prints or digital photos – even video clips – and effortlessly arrange them into exciting, dynamic multimedia shows that play on any CD-R or CD-RW compatible DVD player. See your photos in a whole new way in your own stunning presentation.

Go to www.databecker.com
to order or for more information

Perfect Photo Printer™

ELIMINATE WASTE & MAXIMIZE USE OF EXPENSIVE PHOTO PAPER!

Software for Windows®

PROFESSIONAL PRINTS EVERY TIME!

- 📷 Easily import any popular image file
- 📷 Automatically sizes and positions your images – use built-in templates, access web updates or easily build your own templates
- 📷 Print an index of thumbnails to create your own image catalog
- 📷 Compatible with all major paper manufacturers
- 📷 Includes **FREE** Konica® Photo Inkjet Paper

INSTANT EFFECTS

- 📷 Adjust contrast, sharpness and brightness
- 📷 Remove "red eye"
- 📷 Fix underexposure and overexposure
- 📷 Crop images and create cutouts
- 📷 Rotate images

PRINT PICTURES OF ALL SIZES

- 📷 Wallet, 3x5, 4x6, 5x7, 8x10 and more!
- 📷 Print different sizes of photos on the same page by rotating the paper

Stop wasting time and expensive paper – now there is a simple solution for printing professional quality pictures! Perfect Photo Printer™ is an easy-to-use, superior tool that enhances, sizes, and positions your images for flawless results. Easily import photos right from your digital camera, webcam or scanner. Create prints of all sizes, print different pictures on a single sheet, and utilize all of the space on each piece of photo paper. Now all of your captured memories will be picture perfect – no fuss, no hassle!

Go to www.databecker.com
to order or for more information

Instant Photo Editor™

RESTORE OLD PHOTOGRAPHS & IMPROVE NEW DIGITAL PHOTOS!

Software for Windows®

PROFESSIONAL PRINTS EVERY TIME!

- Easily import any popular image file
- Use images right from your scanner, digital camera or webcam
- **Instant Photo Generator** automatically gives you various versions of your photo with different settings
- Check your progress at any time by right-clicking to instantly view your original photo
- Includes **FREE** Konica® Photo Inkjet Paper

INSTANT EFFECTS

Instantly improve your photos, then save your favorite settings

- **One-Click Optimizer** instantly perfects any image
- Adjust contrast, brightness, saturation and gamma value
- Correct and perfect colors
- Remove "red eye"
- Fix underexposure and overexposure
- Eliminate shadows and sunspots
- Crop images and create cutouts
- Rotate and resize

Restore photos from the past and improve photos from today – now there is a simple solution for creating professional quality pictures! Instant Photo Editor™ is an easy-to-use, superior tool that enhances and corrects your images for flawless results. Easily import photos right from your digital camera, webcam or scanner. Use the One-Click Optimizer to automatically generate a perfect picture. Or edit color and contrast, rotate, retouch and crop just the way you want. Now all of your captured memories will be picture perfect!

Go to www.databecker.com
to order or for more information